History of Poland

A Captivating Guide to Polish History

Free Bonus from Captivating History
(Available for a Limited time)

Hi History Lovers!

Now you have a chance to join our exclusive history list so you can get your first history ebook for free as well as discounts and a potential to get more history books for free! Simply visit the link below to join.

Captivatinghistory.com/ebook

Also, make sure to follow us on Facebook, Twitter and Youtube by searching for Captivating History.

Contents

Introduction

The history of one country is defined by its territory, people, and culture, but Poland presents a unique problem. It is a country whose territory often expanded and contracted and was shared by many groups of people at the same or different times. Thus, Poland was also a very culturally and religiously diverse country. The history of the Polish land is not always the history of the Polish people and vice versa. One of the greatest problems with the history of Poland is that, at one point, the country didn't exist at all. Yet the people were distinctly Polish, and their story should be remembered. Its various people disappeared, too, through ethnic cleansings and genocides that made Poland a very homogenous country. Its culture was obliterated by the partitioning of the Polish territories, world wars, and Soviet-style post-war government.

Difficult as it may be, no one can deny that Poland has a rich and colorful history worthy of study. The land itself lies in the heart of Europe. However, it is precisely the geographical position of Poland that has brought the country so many hardships. Perfectly positioned in the middle, bridging the east and west, it's no wonder Poland attracted the attention of all its mighty neighbors: Germany, the Austro-Hungarian Empire, and Russia. Its history is also closely tied with that of Lithuania, Belorussia, and Ukraine, as well as with the Jewish people.

The history of Poland starts with migrating Slavic tribes who inhabited the region abandoned by the Goths. There they settled and founded Western Slavic communities that would soon transform into a true medieval state. In the 10th century, the first dynasty came to power. The Piasts were to rule Poland for the next five centuries. During the Piast period, Poland adopted Western Christianity and expanded its territories significantly. During the reign of the last Piast, Casimir III the Great, Poland achieved its golden age. This was a period of prosperity, territorial unity, and cultural blossoming. However, Casimir III died without a male heir, and through the marriage of his daughter, the Lithuanian Jagiellonian dynasty would come to rule Poland.

The period between the 14th and 16th centuries brought Poland and Lithuania into a territorial and political union. This was the period of the Polish-Lithuanian Commonwealth. The Commonwealth was one of Europe's largest countries, but the Polish dominated the union and enforced Polish culture on the Grand Duchy of Lithuania. The resentment between the two unequal partners of this union grew stronger over time. The chosen form of government was a noble democracy with an elected monarch heading the country—but without real power. The Polish-Lithuanian Commonwealth ended in the late 18th century when the neighboring countries arranged the partitioning of Poland.

The Russian Empire, Prussia (later Germany), and Austro-Hungarian Empire invaded Poland and divided its territory among themselves. Poland was no more, and the Polish people were forced to live under their three foreign rulers. The country thus developed differently in each region. While the western territories underwent Germanization imposed by Prussia and the Habsburg Empire, the east underwent Russification. The Polish cultural identity had to fight for survival, and it is no wonder it had the greatest success surviving abroad, where the Polish nobles and intelligentsia chose to live in exile. Despite Poland's constant attempts to regain independence through insurgence and revolutions, this would not happen until after the First World War.

The three partitioning powers were significantly weakened after the world war and no longer able to hold their grip on Poland. The country once more emerged as an independent republic, transformed into a modern state. However, Polish freedom lasted only as long as the interwar period. In 1939, it was occupied by Nazi Germany and its ally Russia and again lost its independence. It would remain under this occupation until the end of the Second World War in 1945. During the Second World War, Poland underwent a planned genocide and the extermination of a large portion of its population, most of them Jews. Whole cities were obliterated, and those who survived were treated as slaves. Polish culture, language, and education were suppressed. Those who were lucky enough to escape joined foreign armies and helped liberate Europe from the Nazi regime.

After World War II, Poland emerged once more as a free country. However, as part of the Eastern Bloc, it was transformed into a Soviet satellite state. Communism took the country, and through its Soviet-style regime, it led Poland into poverty, heavy industrialization, collectivization, and censorship of the press, education, and arts. During the Communist period, this central European country was known as the Polish People's Republic. The expulsion, extermination, and migration continued, and Poland was left without its historic ethnic diversity. But by the 1980s, new hope was established with the trade union called Solidarity. The union soon became a center of Polish political opposition that would lead the country into a democratic future. With the collapse of the Eastern Bloc, Poland was finally free to hold its first truly democratic elections and turn its center of attention to the west.

Geographically, it already gravitated towards the developed west, and now it could do so culturally and politically.

Chapter 1 – Poland: The Land and the People

Pomeranian burial urns, 7th century BCE
*Photographed by User:Lillyundfreya CC-BY-SA-3.0; https://en.wikipedia.org/wiki/Bronze-
_and_Iron-Age_Poland#/media/File:Gesichtsurnen.jpg)*

The earliest written record from the part of Europe known today as Poland comes from 965 CE. It was a document written by Ibrahim-ibn-Jakub (Yaqub), a Moorish Jew from Spain who accompanied the Khalif (Caliph) of Cordoba on his journey through central Europe. Ibrahim described the people he met on his travels to Prague and possibly Krakow, including the land of the Slavs and the numerous tribes that inhabited it. But this is not where the history of Poland (or of the Polish people inhabiting this region) starts. They came to the area of the Northern European Plain much earlier, while the region was already inhabited by Celtic and Germanic tribes. The first Slavic tribes were concentrated in southern and southeastern regions, where they were a part of the Przeworsk and Zarubintsy cultures of the 3rd century.

Almost nothing is known about these early Slavic tribes, and it is presumed that they came from the regions of the Polish-Ukrainian border and Western Russia. These were the times of frequent migrations, and in the following centuries, more Slavic tribes came to settle the areas that the Germans and the Celts were leaving. By the 7th and the 8th century, the Western Slav tribes settled in the area between the Oder (Odra in Polish) and Vistula rivers, the heartland of Poland. Even this early in the history of the Western Slavs, they called themselves Polanie (Polanians in English), which meant "people of the open fields." This name is very appropriate considering the flat landscape of the Polish heartland.

The first settlements of the Western Slavs were concentrated around the lake region between Gniezno and Poznan cities. This region was later named Greater Poland (Wielkopolska), and it was distinguished from the southern regions of the Polish realm known as Lesser Poland (Małopolska). Greater Poland is now considered the cradle of the modern Polish state. It is an open country with broad fields and meadows fringed by the thick forests. Situated around River Warta and the many lakes that supply this river with water, Greater Poland has very fertile land. Because of its geography, both agriculture and communication roads developed very quickly.

The city of Krakow is the center of the Lesser Poland region, which leans on the slopes of the Carpathian Mountains to the south. Lesser Poland is a hilly region with several mountain ranges: the High Tatras to the south, the Beskids in the west, the peaks of Cracovian Jura, the Holy Cross Mountains in the north, and the hills of Roztocze National Park to the east. Between these mountains and hills lies the fertile valley of the Vistula and San rivers. The people inhabiting the Carpathians are known as the Highlanders (or the Gorals, from the Polish *Górale*), an ethnic group culturally similar to the Moravian Vlachs. These Highlanders are also settled in Slovakia, Romania, and the Czech Republic. Some even emigrated to the United States; their number is highest in Chicago, where they established the Polish Highlander Association of North America.

The Polish mountains and hills of the south are rich with iron, salt, and uranium, while the lowlands and the valleys are suitable for growing fruit and wine. The region of Lesser Poland hosts some of the most ancient Polish cities, such as Krakow, Lublin, and Sandomierz. But the countryside of Lesser Poland was where the population exploded. The geographical position, abundant resources, and fertile land attracted the pre-industrial society that relied on agriculture. Only after the Industrial Revolution did the population movement to the cities start. During the dominance of the Austro-Hungarian Empire, Lesser Poland was a part of Galicia, a geographical and historical region of parts of Poland and Ukraine.

Mazovia, the region on the middle Vistula, wasn't an integral part of the Kingdom of Poland until 1529. This region was made of gravelly soil and morainic deposits and always had poor drainage, which slowed agricultural development. There were no natural resources of interest in Mazovia, and the whole region was very poor. This is where the modern capital of Warsaw is situated, but the city became prominent only because of its convenience and not its achievements. The city was in the middle of the route between

Krakow (then the Polish capital) and Vilnius (Lithuanian capital). With the creation of the Polish-Lithuanian Commonwealth, it was the natural choice for a capital.

The provinces that form a ring around the Polish heartland have a very erratic historical connection with the country. In the valley of the Oder lies Silesia (Polish: Śląsk, German: Schlesien). This region always aspired to independence. Its ancient connection with Poland was cut in 1339 when Silesia became a part of Bohemia and Austria. In 1740, Silesia was incorporated into Prussia. The region itself is a combination of agriculturally-adequate soil in the south (Lower Silesia) and less fertile but mineral-rich soil in the north (Upper Silesia). The agricultural society of the south were the Slavs, and they always considered themselves more Polish than Silesian. But the industrial north had a German character.

Pomerania (Polish: Pomorze, German: Pommern) also had Slavic origins and was connected to Poland from ancient times. This region, too, spent most of its history influenced by Germany. Sometimes Pomerania was simply under the German sphere of influence, but at other times, its parts were integrated into the German state. The Polish name of the region, Pomorze, means "by the sea" because its shores are washed by the waves of the Baltic Sea. Naturally, the people here were fishermen. But the inner land of Pomerania consisted of wild beech and pine forests, and it was very hard to live and work there. The chief cities of Pomerania, Szczecin and Gdańsk, were incorporated into Poland only in 1945.

Prussia (Prusy) was one of the poorest Polish provinces. Like Pomerania, it also lies on the coast of the cold Baltic Sea. It was a land of dark forests and deep, dark lakes—a remote, unproductive, and undesirable area. The eastern part of Prussia was in the hands of the Teutonic Order until 1525, when it became a Polish fief. The western part overlapped with the region of Pomerania and joined the Kingdom of Poland in 1466. The population of Prussia mainly consisted of German colonists and the Germanized Balts. From

1525, the region was ruled by the German House of Hohenzollern, and it was a duchy, later a state of Brandenburg-Prussia. In 1700, it became the Kingdom of Prussia.

Podlachia is a historic region to the east of Poland which often changed its borders throughout history. Mainly it is notable as a region that separates the heartland of Poland from Belarus and Lithuania. It was often part of a wide region known as Polesia (Pripet Marshes). Only the western part of Polesia concentrated around the Bug River belongs to Poland. The rest of the region is shared by Ukraine and Belarus. Many more regions that were historically part of Poland are not today. Such examples are Volhynia and Podolia, historic regions with undefined boundaries considered part of Ukraine today. Other parts of Ukraine, Belarus, and Lithuania once belonged to Poland, such as Red Ruthenia, concentrated around today's Lviv, and Black Ruthenia, part of modern-day Belarus.

Describing these territories as Polish would be controversial, but the Polish influence there is undeniable. Concentrating only on the ethnic boundaries of Poland would be unhistorical, especially because the whole region of what is today Poland, Lithuania, Belarus, and Ukraine was one multiethnic state. Its citizens were not united by shared blood or a common language but by their common allegiance to the same ruler and his law. In the past, being Polish didn't mean being of a certain ethnic origin. It meant belonging to a certain cultural and political reality, similar to the modern-day term "British." All sorts of people with different ethnic and geographical backgrounds called themselves Polish, but all of this changed in the 20th century. Poland is a state that cannot claim territories outside of its ethnic limits anymore. After the world wars, the superpowers divided Europe along ethnic lines. However, many of the states are still multiethnic territories, and Poland is no exemption.

The geographical position of Poland has made it suitable for the flourishing of life since ancient days. The summer lasts for three months and brings lots of sunshine and warmth. However, summer droughts are rare. The winters are cold, but not cold enough to end all possibility of life; there is no permafrost. Springs are very mild, and there are no major floods, unlike the regions further to the east. Storms are rare but not unknown. All in all, Poland has a mild continental climate and low precipitation, around 559 millimeters or 22 inches. Most of the rain falls during the agricultural months between May and August. Of course, the climate varies depending on the region of Poland. In Silesia, winters are shorter, and the agricultural period lasts over 225 days compared to only 150 in the east.

The first humans settled in the valleys of the Oder and Vistula rivers in the 200th millennium BCE. But findings from the Old Stone Age are very rare. In contrast, the New Stone Age is marked by several cultures that rose between 4000 and 1800 BCE. These cultures were named by the predominant features of the pottery that marked them: Funnel Beaker Culture, the Bell Beaker Culture, or the Pit-Comb Culture. The Bronze Age cultures were named after the locations where they were first discovered. Thus, we have the Unetice Culture (c. 1800-1400 BCE), whose people were excellent bronze and goldsmiths, or the Trzciniec Culture (c. 1600-1200 BCE), whose people formed a patriarchal society that worshiped the sun. The most prominent was the Lusatian Culture (c. 1300-400 BCE), with people who practiced agriculture and trade, mostly with the Danube Basin societies and the people of Scandinavia. They met their end with the first wave of the Scythian invasion at the beginning of the Iron Age.

The Iron Age cultures of Poland thrived until the Middle Ages. Some originated in Bohemia and Slovakia (the Bylany and Puchov Cultures), but most are of local origin. But the task of matching these cultures with separate ethnic groups proved to be very tricky.

One main problem with their proper identification was the biased opinion of Polish and German archeologists and historians. The first stubbornly wanted to prove the Polish origin of the early settlers of the Polish lands, while the second wanted to prove their German origins. The evidence gathered is of little help in this matter, as it is confusing and representative of both ethnic groups.

The third party that joined Poland's archeological evidence was Rome, which shows how far the early Roman Empire reached. Although many Roman items and coins were found in archeological sites as far as Prussia, it seems that the empire didn't reach these regions at least until 178 CE. But the trade the inhabitants of Poland conducted with Danubian Basin settlers brought Roman items into their territory even before the empire was aware of this part of the world. Tacitus (c. 56-120 CE), a Roman historian and politician, was the first to describe the Baltic Sea, although he called it the Suebian Sea. He admitted that was the boundary of Rome's knowledge of the world. He mentioned Germanic tribes settled in the regions of Pomerania (Lemovii and Rugii) and Vistula (Goths). He also mentioned a tribe he called "Vendii," but it is uncertain if he was referring to Germanic Vandals or Slavic Wends. Pliny the Elder was the last to mention the regions of the Baltic coast in his *Natural History*. However, he didn't specify any parts of the Baltic Coast or the people that inhabited them.

For the next six hundred years, there was silence. No written document or record mentioned Poland or the people who inhabited it, but archeological research discovered that the agricultural settlements thrived during this silent period. The Ostrogoths ruled the area between the Baltic and the Black Sea during the second and third century CE, but they gave way to the invading Huns. It is very unlikely that Atilla ever crossed the northern Carpathians and entered the territory that is today Poland. But in the 5th century, when the Huns were retreating, they received the final blow somewhere on the banks of the Vistula

River, where the vengeful Ostrogoths defeated their horde. After the Huns came the Avars, who made the lands north of the Carpathians their tributary lands. But by the 7th century, they lost the control of these territories, which enabled the Slavic migration to continue undisturbed. This was a period of infrequent barbaric attacks in this part of the world, and the Slavs were free to settle and even consolidate their presence in modern-day Poland. Aside from two invasions, the Magyars in the 9th century and the Mongols in the 13th century, the Slavs led very peaceful lives.

Chapter 2 – The Piast Dynasty

Piast Coat of Arms
Wereszczyński, CC BY-SA 4.0;
https://en.wikipedia.org/wiki/Piast_dynasty#/media/File:COA_Piast_dynasty.svg

The story of Piast the Wheelwright (Piast Kołodziej) is a Polish legend that tells of the foundation of the Piast dynasty and links the legendary history of Poland with its recorded history. According to the legend, Piast was a peasant who was chosen to be a prince by the people, who wanted to replace the old and wicked ruler Popiel. Piast was chosen because strange visitors he hosted one day cast a spell on his cellar, making it never run out of food and drink. It is unknown if Piast existed, and modern scholars believe he is the semi-legendary founder of the dynasty. The first recorded king of the Piast dynasty was Mieszko I (c. 930-992), believed to be the great-great-grandson of Piast.

Legends before the time of Piast's rule claim that three Slav brothers named Lech, Czech, and Rus founded the Polish, Czech, and Ruthenian peoples. Another legend speaks of King, who killed a dragon of the Vistula River and built his castle on top of the dragon's cave on Wawel Hill in today's Krakow. These legends are old and impossible to connect to real events. But later evidence suggests that Piast lived during the 9th century and probably ruled over the West Slav tribe, the Polanians. That means Piast was probably alive at the end of the reign of Charlemagne (747-814), the first Holy Roman Emperor, or Alfred the Great of the Anglo-Saxons (c. 848/9-899). This was also the period when Christianity started spreading among the Slav tribes from Rome and Constantinople.

Rising from an enchanted peasant to a ruler of the Polanians, Piast would found a dynasty that would rule for five centuries. But first, the Piast rulers had to unite the neighboring tribes into the Polish Kingdom. The real founders of the Polish monarchy were thus Piast's descendants, such as Mieszko I (r. 930-992), Bolesław II the Generous (r. 1076-1079), Bolesław III Wrymouth (r, 1107-1138), and Władysław I Łokietek (r. 1320-1333). Historians often divide the rule of the medieval Polish monarchs into three periods. The first was a primitive monarchy, from the beginning of the dynasty until the death of Bolesław III Wrymouth. The second lasted from 1138 until 1320, and it was a period of fragmentation, also known as "regionalization." The third period started with the coronation of Władysław I Łokietek, who began the process of reunification.

Early Piast Poland

The rise of the Saxon Empire in the 9th century provoked the emergence of the Piast dynasty from obscurity. The Holy Roman Emperor Otto I also put pressure on the neighboring Slav tribes on the eastern borders of his empire. But soon, he received homage from the Bohemian Prince Premyslid. With the immediate neighbors appeased, Otto wanted to plant German colonies in the areas of Brandenburg and Lusatia. In 961-2, he gained papal approval to make the See of Magdeburg a missionary diocese that would convert the Slavonic lands. (A see is the domain under a bishop's authority.) This diocese even sent a mission to Kievan Rus.

Allied with Boleslaus of Bohemia, Polish Prince Mieszko I accepted Christian baptism. He was aware of the Christian and German supremacy in the region and had no choice but to join them. By willingly joining the Christian world, the Polish ruler avoided the forcible conversion of his people similar to that suffered by his neighbors, the Wends. At the same time, Mieszko I worked to preserve the independence of his lands, as the ambitions of the German Empire were obvious. Yet he was loyal to the emperor and even submitted to the infant Otto III in 984. His successor, Bolesław the Brave (992–1025), became one of the closest associates of the new emperor. In return, Otto III visited the city of Gniezno in 1000, when he confirmed the autonomy of the Polish See. Thus the power and prestige of the Piast dynasty and their Polanian state grew, which would later allow the Piast rulers to defy all the Holy Roman Empire's attempts to absorb Poland.

The territory of Piast Poland was not the same as modern-day Poland. It is very hard to define the Piast Poland borders because the territory this dynasty ruled often changed. Only for a brief time during the reign of Bolesław the Brave did the Piast territories resemble the borders of modern Poland. But he also conquered land as far as the Dnieper and the Danube Rivers, and his realm was larger than Poland today. It is also important to understand that the Polish territory wasn't a united political entity, except for a couple of short interludes, until 1320. Even though Bolesław the Brave conquered some land, he couldn't mark fixed boundaries. The state wasn't a state in the modern sense of central authority over a territory. The land itself was much less important to a ruler in these times than the people who inhabited it. Thus, the Piast princes never described their kingdom in terms of acres and territory but in terms of the people they ruled over.

The Piasts began as rulers of only one of many Slavic tribes inhabiting the region. They gained authority over the Vistulanians, most probably during the reign of Bolesław the Brave, although the exact period is unknown. Piast hold on Pomerania and Silesia was never permanent. They also asserted control over Mazovia but could never assert their dominance over the whole region. Further conquests in Red Ruthenia would come only in the 14th century.

The people ruled by the Piast dynasty had mixed ethnic and cultural origins. They also spoke different Slavic languages, a mixture that would create the Polish language (first recorded in the 12th century).

The history of ecclesiastical Poland proved to be much more straightforward than its political history. Established in the year 1000, the See of Gniezno continued to exist throughout the Middle Ages. But the hierarchy of the church didn't come immediately after the conversion of Mieszko I. Before Gniezno, Poland had only one apostolic bishopric in Poznan. In 991, Mieszko I asked the pope to put his kingdom under the direct protection of Rome. But it was not until the year 1000 that the pope asked Emperor Otto III to visit Gniezno and establish a metropolitan see there. The emperor also elevated Radim Gaudentius, an illegitimate son of Bohemian Prince Slavník, as the first archbishop of Polania. He proceeded to establish bishoprics in Krakow (for Vistulans), Wrocław (for Silesians), and Kolberg (for Pomeranians).

After the death of Bolesław the Brave, the hierarchy of the young Polish church was disrupted by the pagan uprising of the 1030s. Both the state and the church were engulfed in this revolt of the people in reaction to Christianization. Many churches were destroyed during the uprising, and the See of Gniezno was crippled. But it took a mere decade to reconstruct the hierarchy of the Polish Church, which continued uninterrupted from this point in history. With the addition of the new provinces to the kingdom of Poland, new dioceses were opened, and the Poznan church's structure expanded. A parochial network was established in the 12th century, but monasticism in Poland started even earlier, in the 11th century. The first monastic order was the Benedictines, who established their monastery near Poznań. The Cistercians came in the 12th century and strengthened monasticism in Poland.

The relationship between the young church and the early Polish state was not simple. The Piast princes often needed the support of the bishops against ambitious nobles. But on other occasions, the bishops would side with the nobles against the Piast rulers and provoke their reactions. For example, in 1079, King Bolesław II ordered Bishop Stanisław Szczepanowski murdered. This bishop of Krakow had excommunicated the king because of his cruelty and immoral conduct and even organized a rebellion of the nobles. Legend has it that Bolesław personally killed and dismembered the bishop. The martyrdom of Stanisław Szczepanowski only served to anger the nobles, who expelled the king.

The monarchy's status in the early Piast period was never strictly defined. For practical reasons, historians refer to the Poland of this period as a kingdom. But the official title of its rulers was not a king or a prince, but dux (duke), or *herzog* in German. But unlike in western European countries, the title of a duke in Poland never symbolized a certain level of subordination. Germans interpret the title as the Piast dynasty's allegiance to the Holy Roman Empire. But in Polish, the title of a duke is *książę*, and it serves to distinguish an uncrowned prince from the king (*król*). This is how Bolesław III Wrymouth titled his five sons in 1138 when he divided his realm among them. The eldest son was *książę* senior (high duke), and he was superior to his younger brothers, who were only *książę* (duke).

Still, some Polish rulers submitted to the emperor's overlordship, regardless of their title—high duke, duke, or king. In 1033, Mieszko II (r. 1025-1031) submitted to Conrad II (r. 1027-1039) during the Congress of Merseburg, thus making Poland an imperial fiefdom. Mieszko II was crowned king, but that doesn't make him a more significant ruler than his son, Casimir the Restorer (r. 1040-1058), who unified Poland after the pagan rebellion of the 1030s but was never crowned. Coronation was not a condition for the right to rule in early Piast Poland, but some Polish rulers wanted the prestige that came with the crown. The case of Bolesław II the Generous proves that the Piasts didn't need the approval of the emperor to proclaim themselves kings. Bolesław II crowned himself in 1076, while his immediate successor, Władysław I Herman (r. 1079-1102), didn't have a crown even after submitting to the emperor.

The Fragmentation Period

When Bolesław III divided the Polish kingdom among his four oldest sons, he started the period of fragmentation—though he had intended to prevent the brothers from dividing the kingdom or committing fratricide. He made a series of arrangements by which his eldest son would rule as a high duke, and the rest of his sons would be lesser dukes. However, after Bolesław's death, these plans weren't implemented as he intended, and the brothers started fighting for the Polish throne in Krakow. Poland would remain fractured and the coronation of a king impossible.

Bolesław III borrowed the practice of kingdom division from Kyiv. The overall political authority would lie with his eldest son, High Duke Vladislaus the Exile. The high duke had his seat in Krakow, where the Polish throne was, and the provinces of Krakow and Sandomierz were his power base. But he also had the right to represent the whole of Poland in international matters and appoint all the lay and ecclesiastical offices in the country. His younger brothers were dukes of different provinces and acted as the viceroys of the high duke. Each duke was succeeded by his eldest son.

But this partition of the Polish kingdom didn't work as Bolesław III initially planned. In 1202, there were five principalities in Poland, and by 1250, there were nine. The fragmentation continued, and by 1288 there were seventeen provinces, ten of which were in Silesia. This fragmentation happened because of the succession system, in which the younger brothers did not get any territory. They would band together against the eldest brother and start a conflict that would end with the further fragmentation of the provinces into smaller duchies. The lay and ecclesiastical officials often supported the younger brothers, hoping they would be later rewarded for their loyalty. In 1146, High Duke Władysław II the Exile was expelled from Poland, which only deepened the distrust between the members of the Piast dynasty. Władysław II escaped first to Bohemia and then to Germany, where he was received by his brother-in-law, Emperor Conrad III. Although he never returned to Poland, his son, Bolesław the Tall, would return to Silesia in 1163 with the help of Conrad's son Frederick I Barbarossa.

In 1173, Mieszko III the Old (fourth son of Bolesław III Wrymouth with his second wife) became High Duke of Poland. He ruled periodically until 1202. On occasion, he would lose the position of high duke, as many of his family members—even one of his sons—conspired against him and wanted to install Casimir the Just, Duke of Wiślica, on the throne in Krakow.

The fragmentation of Poland into small duchies was very severe, and the fratricide was disturbing. But in all the succession fighting, Krakow never lost its prestigious position as the throne city. No one could claim the title of high duke and impose his authority over Poland without controlling Krakow.

The struggles Poland had during the fragmentation period were due to the unwillingness of the Piast family to follow the rule of the succession of the eldest son. This idea that the high duke should always be the eldest Piast couldn't survive in a society that wanted to elect its own rulers. Casimir the Just was elected high duke by other family members of the Piast dynasty, but even they needed to consult the Krakow-Sandomierz nobility and seek the approval of the ecclesiastical officials.

The fragmentation period was, in a way, paradoxical. On the one hand, the government and administration of Poland were crumbling due to the many small duchies that came into existence. But the economy and culture of the country flourished because of the role of the people and their significance to their rulers. The more people rulers controlled, the more resources they could gain. Many smaller dukes started attracting foreign colonists to their duchies, promising exemptions from taxes and servitude. The prospect of a better life brought new people of various origins who not only worked the land, traded, or manufactured various goods but also brought their culture and traditions, which merged with domestic ones.

Bolesław the Tall and his successor son Henry the Bearded (r. 1232-1238) were in a particularly good position to settle Silesia with colonists. Due to the exile of Bolesław's father, they spent their early lives in Germany. Once back in Silesia, they were able to attract German settlers. These settlers made Silesia a strong and prosperous duchy, and the Piasts of Silesia used this fact to lay claim to the title high duke. The German settlers in Silesia also brought advanced farming techniques, such as compact field systems, technically-improved mills, and heavy plows. By 1229, Germans started dominating Silesia, and Henry the Bearded realized he needed to attract Polish settlers, too—though he never offered them the same level of exemptions and immunities as he had the Germans. Still, the prospect of a better life in rich Silesia was enough for many Poles to come.

With the new settlement policies, Polish cities started blooming, and soon they wanted a certain amount of autonomy. Henry the Bearded was aware of the German city model, in which each had an assembly of aldermen, elected or co-opted, that ran the city's administration. The aldermen who assisted the Vogt (Wójt in Polish) were called magistrates, a title similar to that of a town major today. The magistrates and the Vogt administered the towns according to municipal laws. This model of city and town administration would become almost universal in Poland. But first cities to accept such a self-administration model were Złotoryja in Silesia (1211) and Krakow (1258). At the end of the 13th century, around one hundred Polish cities accepted the German model of self-administration.

But the governing classes in the Polish towns were German, while the Polish people remained peasants. They were forbidden from living in major cities, especially in Krakow, because the princes and nobility didn't want to lose workers from their family estates. The Polish language became the language of the peasantry, while German became the main language of the cities. Some Germanized Polish individuals were allowed to live and work in the cities, and they spoke exclusively German. The only community that resented the Germanization was the Polish clergy. They didn't allow the Germans to join their ranks, fearing Poland would become the new Saxony. The clergy remained the bastion of preservation of the Polish language, traditions, and customs, which they would pass on to ordinary Polish people.

The Polish language wasn't used in sermons until the later 13th century. As a literary medium, it was not sophisticated enough. But, due to encouragement from within the Polish church—especially from officials such as Archbishop Świnka—the language of the peasantry entered the sermon. In the western parts of the country, the Piasts preferred German and were proud of their literary achievements in the language of their neighbors. But in the east, the German language was used only in isolated German communities or bigger towns. There, Polish predominated, as the people were predominantly peasants. Even Germans who settled in the countryside in the east used Polish in their day-to-day lives. The case was the same with German knights who came to serve the Polish courts.

Reunification

Portrait of Władysław I Łokietek
https://commons.wikimedia.org/wiki/File:Wladyslaw_Lokietek.jpg#mw-jump-to-license

The church in Poland had an interest in keeping the country united, and it was a victim of the political fragmentation of the realm. After the dukes, the church was the principal landowner, and further fragmentation would divide church-owned land. But external threats to the small and insecure duchies played an even bigger role in stopping Poland's fragmentation. Many dukes found themselves incapable of defending their realms from still-pagan Slavic tribes and the Mongols. The Duchy of Masovia suffered continuous attacks from Prussia, and to counter these, its Duke Conrad settled the Teutonic Knight order in the area of lower Vistula. But not all dukes could afford to invite the Crusade knights to their land for various political and cultural reasons. They had to suffer through the devastating onslaught of the Mongols, who swept across Poland in 1241. Only the death of the Great Khan Ogedei of the Mongols could stop the invasion and force the horde into retreat. But they remained in the plains of the Eastern Balkans and the Black Sea area and would continue to harass the Polish dukes with frequent raids.

The first Piast who started the road of reunification was Henryk IV Probus (c. 1258-1290), Duke of Silesia and Wrocław and later High Duke. He started negotiating with the papacy and Holy Roman Emperor Rudolf I to receive a crown. This step was far from Poland's reunification, but it was a symbolically important one. Unfortunately, Henryk died before being crowned, and he had no successors. As he was childless, Henryk dedicated the office of high duke to Przemysł II in his will. Przemysł II already possessed Gdansk and was a duke of eastern Pomerania. With the office of high duke, he received control over the province of Krakow. This meant that Przemysł II had control of a much greater power base than any other Polish duke or any of his predecessors.

The only rival Przemysł II had was Władysław I Łokietek, duke of Łęczyca, Sieradz and Kuyavia. In 1289, Władysław also received the office of high duke—not from Henryk (who was chosen by the townsmen of Krakow) but from his cousin, Duke Bolesław II of Masovia (chosen by the nobles, knights, and the bishop of Krakow). Conflict between the two pretenders to the office loomed but never happened. Little is known about the relations between the two dukes. While Przemysł II stayed in Krakow, Władysław remained in Sandomierz. Although these two territories were inseparable as the possessions of the high duke, now they were divided, and both Przemysł and Władysław claimed them.

Both Przemysł and Władysław were overshadowed by the events in Poland brought forth by a foreign ruler, Wenceslaus II of Bohemia. In 1290, Przemysł II left Krakow with Polish regalia, obviously planning to crown himself. Wenceslaus II wanted to acquire Lesser Poland, and it helped that he had the support of local barons and nobles. He had far more to offer them in terms of wealth, prestige, and military power than either Władysław or Przemysł II. Przemysł knew that he could not fight the superior Bohemian army and agreed to cede Lesser Poland to Wenceslaus. Władysław I Łokietek fought briefly but was quickly abandoned by his knights and had to surrender control over Sandomierz.

However, in 1295, Przemysł II was crowned in Gniezno cathedral by Archbishop Świnka, who personally persuaded the pope to approve this coronation. But it remains unclear if Przemysł II became king of the entirety of Poland or only of Greater Poland and Pomerania. Nevertheless, he didn't live long after the coronation, as he was killed approximately eight months later. The barons of Greater Poland wanted Władysław I Łokietek as his successor, but his willingness to divide the new kingdom with other Polish dukes resulted in the loss of support. When in 1299 he officially acknowledged Wenceslaus II as his overlord, it was obvious that the Bohemian king was the right choice for the Polish crown. Even Archbishop Świnka couldn't do anything to stop this coronation, which he conducted in September 1300.

With King Wenceslaus II receiving the Polish Crown, Poland was reunited, though much of the territory remained in the hands of small dukes. The Bohemian king directly controlled Greater Poland, Krakow-Sandomierz, and eastern Pomerania. Wenceslaus didn't intend to unite all of Poland. He considered his Polish territories to be subordinate to his Bohemian ones. Because of this, many of his Polish subjects started resenting him. Władysław I Łokietek was exiled, and he had no choice but to search for support among foreign rulers. He even went to Rome, where Pope Boniface VIII received him. The pope was already hostile toward the Bohemian king and had no trouble supporting the Polish pretender to the throne.

The resentment of the people intensified during the next few years. The Hungarian throne was empty in 1301 when King Andrew III died without an heir. Wenceslaus II of Bohemia wanted to install his eleven-year-old son on the throne of Hungary, but the people wouldn't allow it. By 1304, Hungary and Germany formed a coalition to fight the Bohemian claim over the Hungarian throne. To appease them, Wenceslaus of Bohemia wanted to give eastern Pomerania and Gdansk to the Margraves of Brandenburg, but the Polish nobles wouldn't let this happen. In 1305, a revolt started with the nobles of eastern Pomerania wanting to install Henry III, Duke of Głogów as the king of Poland. But the Hungarian-German coalition pushed for the return of Władysław Łokietek from exile and his coronation. With the help of foreign armies, Łokietek seized all the territories of Lesser Poland except the city of Krakow.

The Bohemian king died in 1305, and his son and successor, Wenceslaus III of Bohemia, continued his father's policy. He reconciled with the Hungarian-German coalition and again offered to surrender Gdansk and Pomerania to the Margraves of Brandenburg. But in 1306, Wenceslaus III was murdered by discontent Bohemian nobles. Bohemia would remain in succession until 1310. In Poland, Łokietek seized the opportunity to take

Krakow. But Greater Poland remained under the control of Henry of Głogów. As for Gdansk, Margraves Otto and Waldemar besieged the city, intending to take it by force. Łokietek was unable to defend the city with his army, and he called the Teutonic Knights for help. The knights came and broke the siege, but they also turned against Łokietek and his army and took the Castle of Gdansk for themselves. In just one year, most of Pomerania fell into the hands of the Teutonic Order.

Although Władysław Łokietek kept control of Lesser Poland and some territories in Pomerania, he was unable to gain the nobles' trust. When the Germans of Krakow rebelled in 1311, he was able to subdue them only with the help of the Hungarian army. He replaced all the German officials with Poles, and Latin was used for city record keeping instead of the German language. The German presence weakened, and Krakow ceased being the political center it once was. Łokietek was not the favorite choice of the rulers of the nobles in other towns. However, they still preferred him to the Germanized sons of Henry of Głogów, who would succeed him after his death in 1309. The five sons of Głogów would only continue the fragmentation of Poland. At this time, Łokietek proved his aspiration to become king of a united Poland. But he had yet to deal with competition from the new king of Bohemia, John of Luxembourg.

Brandenburg, the Teutonic Knights, and Silesian and Masovian dukes supported the Bohemian king. But he needed to persuade the reluctant Pope John XXII to give him approval for a coronation. The pope consented to the coronation but didn't specify whose: he considered both throne pretenders legitimate. To avoid angering his rival, John of Luxembourg, Łokietek was crowned in Krakow, in 1320, as King of Poland. However, since John of Bohemia also used the title King of Poland internationally, Łokietek was regarded as having control over only Krakow Province.

Corona Regni Poloniae

Władysław I Łokietek strengthened his position as a Polish king with marriage alliances. In 1320, he married his daughter, Elizabeth, to King Charles Robert of Hungary. Five years later, he arranged a marriage between his second son (later King Casimir III) and Princess Aldona of Lithuania. By having such powerful allies, Łokietek was safe from John of Luxembourg, who planned an attack on Krakow. But the main trouble Łokietek had was with the Teutonic Knights, who had earlier seized Pomerania. The Bohemian king joined the Knights, and together they managed to take the northern territory of Poland, known as Dobrzyń Land. John then used his claim over the Polish throne to give this land to the Knights.

John of Luxembourg now had the support of all Silesian dukes and Duke Wenceslaus of Płock, who suffered an attack from Łokietek in 1325. The reasons for this attack remain unknown, but it was certainly an event that pushed Wenceslaus to support his cousin, the Bohemian king. Due to his connection to John, Wenceslaus joined the Teutonic Knights against Łokietek in 1326, when the Polish-Teutonic War started (lasted until 1332). During the war, both sides successfully took some of the Polish territories. But the last battle, the Battle of Płowce in 1331, proved indecisive. Although Władysław I Łokietek and his son Casimir had the advantage in numbers, they proved to be inadequately equipped to fight the well-trained and wealthy army of the Teutonic Knights. The father and son were forced to flee the battlefield and sue for an armistice.

Although there were no more battles, the war officially ended with the Peace of Kalisz, signed in 1343 by Casimir III, Władysław's son. With this peace, the Polish king received the territories of Kuyavia and Dobrzyń but lost Pomeralia (eastern Pomerania) to the Teutonic Knights. Władysław I Łokietek was already ill and weak during the Polish-Teutonic War, and in 1333, he finally died. The kingdom he left to his son was smaller than the one he had gained with the coronation in Krakow. Casimir ruled over a narrow and elongated territory along the Vistula River. This area, which had approximately 800,000 people, was a small kingdom and could hardly be associated with Poland today. Nevertheless, the *Corona Regni Poloniae* was established by Casimir and his jurists. This meant that the Crown of the Polish Kingdom existed separately from the monarch, and Poland was no longer private possession of the Piast dynasty.

Casimir III (r. 1333-1370) proved to be much more a diplomat and statesman than a warrior. Upon his succession to the throne, he promulgated a truce with the Teutonic Knights and turned to the domestic matters of Poland. First, he needed to strengthen royal authority; only then could he turn to crucial external matters, such as relations with the Teutonic Order and John of Luxembourg. Casimir had no help in the matter of the Knights. His father's allies, the Hungarian Angevins, were unwilling to resume conflict with the Order, as they had their own issues with Luxembourg and the German House of Wittelsbach. Losing the alliance with Hungary, Casimir III had no choice but to give up on Pomerania in the Peace of Kalisz of 1343.

Casimir also had to accept the loss of Silesia when, in 1348, it was incorporated into the Kingdom of Bohemia. In 1355, Duke Siemowit III of Masovia acknowledged his overlordship. However, the Masovian duke made it clear that the relationship with Casimir would extend after his death only if the king provided a male heir. Casimir's abandonment of the territories in the west can be explained by the development of events on the eastern border of his kingdom. Kievan Rus had experienced the same fragmentation as Poland, and the many principalities became tributaries of the Golden Horde (the Tartar and Mongol army). The two westernmost principalities, Volhynia and Galicia, were ruled by Piast King Yuri II Boleslav of Ruthenia. He had no children and wanted to name Casimir III of Poland as his successor. For this, he was poisoned by his boyar advisers.

Because no credible Rus prince claimed the Ruthenian territories, Casimir III seized the opportunity to claim them. These territories were not only fertile but also on the main merchant route from Germany to the Black Sea. Whoever controlled them could look forward to the riches he could claim from the merchant taxes. Another advantage of the territory was that it could serve as a buffer zone between Poland and the raiding Tartars. Ruthenia and the territories of Volhynia and Galicia were great compensation for the loss of the western territories of Silesia and Pomerania, but it wouldn't be so simple for Casimir to annex these territories. To impose Polish authority over them, he had to fight for the next twenty years. The result of the struggle was Lithuanian establishment in the north, while Poland held the southern territories centered around today's Lviv.

In the Lithuanian northern Ruthenia, the seven sons of Duke Gediminas fought for control of the territory upon his death in 1341. Casimir III saw the advantage in this and started preparing for the conquest. But to raise money for the war effort, he had plundered the treasury of the Gniezno archbishopric. This proved insufficient, so the Polish king had to borrow money from all the dukes and even the Teutonic Knights. To secure the Knight's investment, Casimir III gave them the territory of Dobrzyń, an impoverished countryside that couldn't compare to the prosperity that would come with the control of Ruthenia. The endeavor proved successful, and Casimir III took control of the northern parts of Ruthenia from Lithuania, completely controlling the trade route to the Black Sea.

By creating *Corona Regni Poloniae*, Casimir III wanted to restore a strong monarchic rule in Poland. To do this, he needed educated Polish advisers from the southern territories to replace the existing German ones. The king needed to create a new level of society composed of educated Polish people. In 1364, he founded the first Polish university known as *studium generale* in Krakow. (This university still operates as Jagiellonian University, one of the oldest universities in the world.) The first courses of the university were law, medicine, and astronomy. The state's need for doctors, jurists, and lawyers dictated the early curriculums. Casimir also introduced many reforms in the Polish judicial system and approved the new civil and criminal code.

Unlike other European rulers of the period, Casimir III was not an anti-Semite. In 1334, he granted some privileges to the Jews and actively sought to settle them in his territory. Although the people of Poland didn't agree with their king on this matter, Jews were allowed to settle and work either in the towns' suburbs or in Jewish enclaves. Conflict between Catholic Polish people and the Jews was unavoidable, as many local merchants and bankers feared for their businesses. However, these conflicts never escalated to revolt and never had Casimir's support. The king prohibited the forceful Christianization of kidnapped Jewish children and the desecration of Jewish cemeteries. Legend has it that Casimir had a Jewish mistress named Esterka, but this information was never historically confirmed.

In 1338, Casimir introduced coinage reform, and small silver coins started circulating in Poland. This and the development of trade with Krakow in the center of Poland enabled Casimir to pursue a harsher fiscal policy for the kingdom. With the introduction of a new annual land tax and the income from the salt mines of Bochnia and Wieliczka, Casimir started defense reconstruction in many towns and citadels. He built around fifty new castles and citadels across Poland and raised walls around twenty-seven towns. With these extensive building projects, he secured the land from Tatar invasions and raids from Lithuania.

Casimir III is the only Polish king honored with the title "The Great." His achievements elevated Poland to a medieval European kingdom, though it remained small and without much influence on the international political scene. His reforms, establishment of the university, and building program are celebrated to this date. But Casimir III failed in one area: he didn't have a male heir. The Polish king married four times, but with two of his wives, he had only daughters, and the other two marriages were childless. In 1355, Casimir proclaimed his nephew Louis I of Hungary as his heir, as he was still hoping a son would come. But he didn't want to leave his kingdom to a foreign ruler, and in 1368, he named his grandson, Casimir IV of Pomerania, as his heir. The child was born to his eldest daughter Elisabeth, and the succession plans were set in place.

But when Casimir died in 1370, Louis I of Hungary personally traveled to Krakow, where he bribed and persuaded the nobles to annul Casimir's proclamation of succession and choose him instead. So it happened that the Polish Kingdom came into the hands of the Hungarian ruler. However, much of the political power was actually in the hands of Louis's mother Elizabeth, sister of Casimir III the Great. She managed to prevent the fragmentation of Poland by allowing Casimir IV to control the Dobrzyń Land as compensation. The Polish nobles welcomed the rule of the foreign king because it meant he would be absent and never take an active role in domestic politics.

But Louis I of Hungary proved equally unable to father a son and an heir. Unlike his predecessor, in 1374, Louis managed to persuade the Polish nobles to accept one of his daughters as an heiress. To achieve this, he had to agree to many concessions and favors and reduced taxes for nobles, clergy, and peasants. These concessions made the Polish nobles a dominant power within the state. But Louis never really intended to keep Poland an independent kingdom. In 1377, he incorporated Polish Rus lands into the Kingdom of Hungary. He also confirmed Luxembourg's right to Silesia and granted some border land to Brandenburg. This made Hungarian rule very unpopular among the Polish. The oppressive behavior of Hungarian officials in Krakow only strengthened the resentment towards Louis. The culmination of the estranged relations ended with a massacre during the riots in Krakow in 1376.

When Louis I of Hungary died in 1382, the nobles were no longer interested in supporting any of his daughters as legitimate heirs in Poland. They had previously agreed to declare Louis's daughter Maria their queen, but once he proposed her marriage to Sigismund of Luxembourg, they withdrew their support. The Hungarian nobles then proposed Louis's younger daughter Jadwiga, and while Lesser Poland agreed to this, Greater Poland refused. Their choice for the Polish Crown was Duke Siemowit IV of Płock, but the duke withdrew under the threat of Angevine troops stationed in southern Poland.

Jadwiga was crowned in Krakow on October 15, 1384, under the condition that her engagement to the Wilhelm of Habsburg be broken. The nobles of Greater Poland wanted her married to Siemowit IV. But that didn't happen, as the nobles of Lesser Poland wouldn't agree. Instead, Jadwiga was married to the pagan Lithuanian Duke Jogaila. According to the promises he made by signing the Act of Kreva, Jogaila was baptized and crowned in Krakow in 1386. He was also obliged to spread Christianity among his pagan subjects. As a king of Poland, he changed his name to Władysław Jagiełło and started his reign as Jadwiga's co-ruler. With this marriage, Poland annexed the Lithuanian duchy, a vast territory stretching from the Baltic to the Black Sea.

Chapter 3 – Poland Under the Jagiellonian Dynasty

Jagiellonian Coat of Arms
Wereszczyński, CC BY-SA 4.0;
https://en.wikipedia.org/wiki/Jagiellonian_dynasty#/media/File:COA_Jagiellon.svg

With the coronation of Jogaila, Grand Duke of Lithuania, and his marriage to Jadwiga of Poland, it became clear that the new power had arrived in Europe. Some rulers recognized this and moved their allegiance from Hungary and Bohemia to Poland. The first to do so was Peter (Petru) I Mushat of Moldavia in 1387. Only one century later, both Hungary and Bohemia came under the rule of the Jagiellonian kings. But how did the Jagiellonian king of pagan Lithuania come into the position to spread across Europe and assert Lithuania's dominance over some of Europe's strongest kingdoms? The very existence of Lithuania was threatened just several years before the marriage between Jogaila and Jadwiga. The Teutonic Knights sacked Vilnius (capital of Lithuania) and took the stronghold of Trakai. The western part, known as Samogitia, was ceded to the Knights by Vytautas, Jogaila's cousin and main rival for the office of Grand Duke. The union with Poland through marriage with Jadwiga was Lithuania's desperate attempt to strengthen its position against its internal enemies and the Teutonic Order.

At the time, Lithuania stretched from the Baltic in the north to the Black Sea in the south and from the upper Volga in the west to the territories beyond the Dnieper in the east. The state of Lithuania was always politically unstable, but it was formed by Baltic rulers in the wake of the Mongol attacks of the 13th century. A century later, native pagan Lithuanians numbered no more than 300,000 and were significantly outnumbered by foreign settlers, mainly Christians. The ruling house of Gediminas was the first to convert to Christianity, but the influences came from both the west and east. Some members of the royal household converted to Orthodox Christianity to assert their influence over the Rus lands. The Jagiellonian dynasty was an auxiliary dynasty of Gediminas. Influenced by Poland, they converted to the Catholic faith. After his baptism, Jogaila returned to Lithuania, accompanied by his new wife, and founded the diocese of Vilnius in an attempt to convert his subjects.

The Polish-Lithuanian Union

By accepting Catholicism, Jogaila and his Lithuanian knights hoped they would contain the Teutonic threat, at least to some extent. The union with Poland secured this containment, as now Lithuania had a strong ally on its side. Jogaila never intended to convert the Orthodox Lithuanians to the Catholic faith—only the pagan ones. But to gain the support of his boyars, Jogaila had to give them the same rights and privileges the Polish nobles had, and he did so as soon as 1387. But the reality was different because Jogaila wished for Poland to be his ally against his cousin Vytautas as much as against the Teutonic Order. To keep the Poles interested in fighting against his domestic enemy, he had to keep Lithuanians out of the Polish offices. He went even further and gave some of the Lithuanian offices to the nobles of Lesser Poland. He also brought the Polish army to occupy some Lithuanian strongholds. But the fault for this didn't lie only with Jogaila's inability to keep his word. Lithuania lacked judicial institutions, town assemblies, and cultural traditions which would enable them to assume the Polish offices.

The Act of Kreva that Jogaila signed in 1385 obliged him to return the lands previously controlled by Poland but lost to its enemies. This referred to Pomerania, now in the hands of the Teutonic Knights. But Poles were most certainly more interested in gaining the fertile lands of Galicia, which were once subdued by Casimir III and now belonged to Lithuania. They even hoped that Lithuania would be quickly incorporated into Poland. This was a matter on which the Polish nobles insisted for over 150 years. But Jogaila and his successors regarded incorporation as a tactical promise that could be avoided and acted accordingly. Poland and Lithuania continued existing as a union, signed over and over again, not only in Kreva but also in Vilnius (1401), Horodlo (1413), Grodno (1432), and again Vilnius (1499). The many different unions were signed in the attempt to redefine the relationship between Poland and Lithuania, all in light of changing political circumstances.

The Lithuanians appreciated the dynastic union with Poland but were eager to retain a high level of independence. In contrast, Poland always sought to influence and dominate the Grand Duchy, if not to completely annex it. The final results of different unions and unification acts were often contradicting compromises, always left open to various interpretations. Even modern historians argue over them and the meaning they carried for Poland and Lithuania. For example, the Union of Horodlo from 1413 explicitly called for the joining of Lithuania to the Crown of Poland but continued to treat the two as separate states. The Union of Vilnius from 1499 confirmed the Union of Horodlo, but it did so in a way that the incorporation was left out. Moreover, the Vilnius Union suggested a common election by the nobles and lords of Poland and Lithuania, but the formal and legal machinery that would promulgate the elections was never set in place. Although the relationship between the two states was confusing, the situation it created seemed to suit the Jagiellonian dynasty. The Grand Duchy of Lithuania was their hereditary land, and that fact made them the only candidates for the Polish Crown.

In 1396, Jadwiga and her husband annexed a belt of territories that separated Lesser Poland from Greater Poland. These narrow territories had been granted to Vladislaus II of Opole, a Silesian Piast, by Louis I of Hungary. Jadwiga decided to annex Vladislaus's lands because, in 1392, he schemed to divide Poland between the Teutonic Knights and their Ordensstaat (a separate Teutonic state) and Sigismund of Hungary (who would later become Holy Roman Emperor). Jadwiga also managed to return some of the Rus territories previously taken by Hungary and some of the territories of extinct Piast lords, namely in Masovia. The Polish lands expanded, but the process was very slow. Poland would not gain the territories around Warsaw, its modern-day capital, until 1526.

Silesia and Pomerania remained out of reach, and the Polish Crown wasn't strong enough to enforce the annexation of Lithuania, whose lords actively sought to keep union with Poland but with a high level of autonomy. The result was that after some time, the two countries pursued different (and often conflicting) foreign policies. Poland always looked to the north and south for further expansion, while Lithuania wanted to expand to the east. The relationship between the two states deteriorated even more when the lords of Lithuania chose Jogaila's second son, Casimir, as their Grand Duke, while his first son Władysław III ruled as Polish king. But relations were repaired after the death of Władysław at the Battle of Varna in 1444. After a short interregnum, Casimir III was crowned king in 1447. A similar thing happened in 1492, when John Albert, Jogaila's grandson, was elected king while his brother, Alexander, was the Grand Duke of Lithuania. The union was back in place by 1501 when Alexander became king, as his older brother had no successors.

Poland-Lithuania Against Ordensstaat

The conflict between Poland and the Teutonic Knights began officially in 1409 when Jogaila started openly persuading the Polish lords to fight the Knights. Before that, Poland fought the order unofficially by sending volunteers to serve in the Lithuanian army of Jogaila's cousin Vytautas. The Grand Master of the Teutonic Knights, Ulrich von Jungingen, responded to Jogaila's warmongering by attacking the northern territories of Poland. The long conflict, known as the Polish-Lithuanian-Teutonic War, began in 1409. Although it officially ended in 1411, the conflict was not truly resolved until 1466, when the territories the order had seized during the reign of Władysław I Łokietek were regained. The grand victory for the Polish-Lithuanian union came at the Battle of Grunwald in 1410, but their army failed to take over the Teutonic capital Marienburg (today's Malbork). The Knights were safe behind the walls of their city because Poland didn't have the means to sustain a prolonged siege.

A series of wars followed in 1414, 1422, and 1431-35, which didn't bring any new territory to Poland. But Lithuania managed to restore Samogitia in 1422. Vytautas was satisfied with this gain and ceased helping Poland against the Teutonic Knights. Instead, he concentrated on conquering the Rus lands. But the constant warfare weakened the Knights as their Prussian possessions were devastated. To compensate for their losses, the Teutonic order installed some brutal fiscal policies and pushed their subjects into a revolt. It didn't help that Germany was experiencing a political and demographic crisis at the time and was unable to send men to the Order. In 1464, the Polish Crown issued an act that incorporated Prussia. But the Crown did so with the approval of the Prussian nobility and representatives of the great cities such as Danzig (Gdansk), Elbing (Elbląg), and Thorn (Toruń).

The subjects of the Ordesstaat were defecting in great numbers. It even seemed as if Poland would win back its territories without a fight. But the Teutonic Order managed to survive, and the Polish treasury started weakening. When another war erupted between Poland and the Knights in 1454, Casimir III could barely afford 2,000 mercenaries. The Knights were no better off financially, and the war dragged on for the next thirteen years. The financial drain was such that the people started complaining about how the war cost the Polish Crown much more than Prussia's worth. In 1457, the Polish finally took over the Marienburg castle, but peace would come only in 1466.

Signed in Thorn on October 19, the peace displayed how weak the Teutonic Order had become by the end of the war. It had to cede the territories along the lower Vistula River, which became Royal Prussia. They also lost the rich see of Warmia, which became a separate principality under the control of the Polish Crown. But the Order managed to keep the port of Königsberg (now

Kaliningrad, Russia)—not-so-rich land. The grand master of the Order was also obliged to pay homage to the Polish king. Although the Peace of Thorn was a success for Poland, as it managed to incorporate Prussia, the province remained autonomous, and its nobles regarded it as a separate political entity. Various grand masters worked tirelessly to reverse the Peace of Thorn and lose the vassal status they had. Some even managed to avoid paying homage to the Polish king.

These refusals led to yet another conflict in 1519, which ended by 1521 with an inconclusive truce. The situation was resolved by an intervention, a *deus ex machina* that came in the form of the religious rebellion of Martin Luther. In 1525, Grand Master Albrecht von Hohenzollern-Ansbach, a Lutheran himself who supported the reform of the church, used his religious stance to propose the secularization of the Order in Prussia to King Sigismund I of Poland (1506-1548). The 1525 Treaty of Krakow made eastern Prussia a duchy and a hereditary land of the grand master. But it would revert to the Polish principality if his line became extinct. The few Order members agreed to this because they saw the opportunity to elevate themselves from the financial hole the Order was in due to all the wars.

The Jagiellonian Interests in the South

The difficulties in the north contrasted with the Polish successes in the south. At the end of the 14th century, the royal authority in Hungary and Bohemia corroded. The Luxemburg Dynasty had no male successors, and the sisters of Polish Queen Jadwiga, Mary and Hedwig, died without leaving any children behind. The Jagiellonians sought to acquire Hungary and Bohemia because they didn't want the neighboring kingdoms to fall into the hands of their enemies. The Polish nobles remembered the Angevin and Luxembourg support of the Teutonic Knights and wanted to spread their influence on Hungarian and Bohemian lands. The regency council that ruled the country after the death of Jogaila tried to put his son, Władysław III, onto the Hungarian throne in 1440. They gravely miscalculated, and their actions led to a civil war. To end this domestic conflict, the council pushed Władysław's supporters and opponents into a crusade against the Ottoman Turks. Władysław III led his army and found his death at the battle of Varna in 1444. The battle would be a complete loss for the Christian army if not for the capable leadership of Hungarian nobleman John Hunyadi.

When the Polish-Lithuanian Jagiellonian dynasty eventually took Hungary, it wasn't direct. They had to do it through Bohemia. There was constant conflict in Bohemia between Hussites and Catholics, nobles and land magnates. Events escalated, and they started searching for outside allies. In 1469, to secure the Polish alliance, Bohemian nobles chose the son of Casimir IV, Władysław, as their king-designate. Władysław ascended the Bohemian throne two years later. Hungarian nobles chose him as their ruler in 1491, after the death of their King Mattias Corvinus (r. 1548-1490), the second son of John Hunyadi.

Polish King Casimir IV wanted his younger and favorite son, John Albert, to be elected Hungarian king. This is where the Jagiellonian dynasty displayed its fracture. Władysław II wasn't elected as King of Poland, but his younger brother was. John Albert, King of Poland, wasn't elected Grand Duke of Lithuania, but the youngest of the brothers, Alexander, was. Instead of integrating Bohemia and Hungary into the Polish-Lithuanian union, the leaders allowed their personal ambitions to take advantage. But no matter how troubled the internal relations of the Jagiellonian dynasty were, they did not compare to the troubles the Ottoman Empire presented.

With the fall of Constantinople in 1453, it became clear that the Ottomans posed a threat to all of Europe. Poland was surrounded by Ottoman vassal states—first the Tatars of Crimea, who allowed the Turks to establish garrisons in their coastal towns, and then the southern neighbors Wallachia and Moldavia. Since the accession of Jogaila, Moldavia was a Polish vassal state, but with the coming of the Ottomans, it was clear it would be difficult to keep it in the same position. Moldavia was a small, non-threatening country surrounded by powerful neighbors Hungary, Poland, and the Ottoman Empire. To survive, it had to side with whoever appeared the strongest at a given moment. At one point, the prince of Moldavia, Stephen the Great (r. 1457-1504), had to pay a great amount of money to show his loyalty to the great sultan of the Ottomans just so his lands would not be raided.

Poland and Hungary were rivals, and both wanted to assert their control over Moldavia. This prevented them from cooperating and fighting the Ottomans in the region together. Both countries tried to help Moldavia at separate times and under separate terms. This led to some gains for Moldavia on the coast of the Black Sea, mainly in the port towns of Kilia and Akerman (Belgorod). But at other times, due to a lack of help, these towns were lost to the Ottomans. When the Polish Crown agreed to a truce with the Turks, the Moldavians were furious because that meant they had to acknowledge Polish suzerainty and pay tribute to the Ottomans simultaneously.

The Moldavians rose against the Polish and tried to take the border region of Pokucie. In 1497, Polish king John Albert led his army into Moldavia under the pretense of trying to take over Kilia from the Turks. But instead of doing just that, he also laid a siege to Moldavia's capital Suceava. He intended to install his younger brother, Sigismund, on the Moldavian throne. But this effort of the Polish king proved to be futile. He had to lead his army, which suffered many losses, into a retreat. The Moldavians intensified their raids on Pokucie. John Albert had only managed to make an enemy of his neighboring (and sometimes vassal) state. The relationships with Moldavia would remain a thorn in the Polish side until 1538, when Suleiman the Magnificent took Moldavia under vassalage and asserted strict control over it.

The troubles with Moldavia were grievous, but they were nothing compared to the problems created by the Tatars of Crimea. The Mongol Golden Horde broke up into many khanates around the lower Volga and the Crimea during the 15th century. The Jagiellonian dynasty wanted good relations with these khanates because they were immediate neighbors of their Lithuanian territory. They even tried to influence the Tatars and maneuver them against Moscow. But when Crimea submitted to Ottoman rule in 1475, the Tatars started raiding all their neighbors so they could sell the plunder and slaves in Constantinople and Kaffa (Feodosia, Crimea). In the last decade of the 15th century, the Tartar raids led to the depopulation of huge tracts of Lithuanian Rus lands. In 1482, they reached Kyiv, sacked the city, and left it in ruins. In 1505, they reached Vilnius but managed to sack only the outskirts of the city.

In 1490, the Tatars started raiding deeper in Poland than ever before and went as far as Lublin. Only ten years later, they came close enough to Warsaw to threaten the city's destruction. This Tatar threat was one reason Poland was often unable to send help to its vassal state Moldavia. The Tatars were an enemy impossible to defeat because they were very mobile and hardy. The only damage the Polish army could hope to achieve was while the Tatars were running away with the plunder and slaves that slowed them down. Occasionally, the Polish and Lithuanian armies would win a victory against the Tartars, but they could do nothing to stop the raids.

During the 1490s, Lithuania lost control over its Black Sea territories and stopped its efforts to colonize the area around the eastern bank of the Dnieper River. All this was due to the intensity of the Tartar raids. Even Khan Mengli admitted how his people turned the territory of Ukraine into a wasteland. At the time, Ukraine, which means "borderlands" (Ukraina), referred only to the land between Kyiv and the Polish border. Poland started paying protection money to the Crimean khans. Although less intense, the raids continued as many of the khans admitted they could not control the freebooting of their subjects.

The Tartar raids diminished during the reign of Sigismund II (r. 1548-1572) because he improved the state of many garrisons and fortifications in Polish and Lithuanian-controlled Ukraine. At the same time, the Cossacks established themselves in the region. Existing at least since the 14th century, they were a semi-military self-governing community of adventurers, runaways, petty nobles, or simply free men. The Cossacks had no ethnicity and had complete religious freedom in their society (though later they became exclusively Christian). Because they acted as mercenaries on occasion, many kings and grand dukes patronized them and financed their raids into the Tatar territories. The Cossacks were fierce warriors who could be controlled only by those who earned their respect. Their activity helped deter Tatar raids from Poland and Lithuania and direct them towards Moscow.

The foreign policies of the Polish Jagiellonian dynasty were most ambitiously displayed in the matters of Lithuania's northern and eastern borders. To the north lay the Livonian Order, a territory owned by the Teutonic Order's sister organization, the Knights of the Sword. These territories were mainly Lutheran, and the allegiance of the Knights was with the Holy Roman Emperors. Although Livonia was a rich country due to merchant taxes on the import and export of goods from Lithuania and the Grand Duchy of Moscow, it was politically unstable. The reason for this instability was the relationship of the Knights with the Archbishop of Riga and their constant disagreements. Ivan IV, better known as Ivan the Terrible, always regarded Livonia as part of his Rurikid dynasty's heritage. He saw the quarrels between the Knights and the archbishop as a perfect opportunity to try and take it. But Sigismund II Augustus of Poland (r. 1548-1572), the last Polish ruler of the Jagiellonian dynasty, was also interested in Lavonia because it had rich cities that might provide new revenues.

Sigismund planned to impose vassalage on Livonia, but he didn't have the means for prolonged warfare. His nobles were not ready to finance a war that would not bring the territory of Livonia completely under Polish dominion. But that was out of the question because Lithuanian nobles claimed Livonia as part of their Grand Duchy. Although Sigismund eventually gathered finances to build up impressive artillery, the war didn't happen. Instead, a series of diplomatic understandings between Livonia and Poland occurred, and in 1561, this territory was made an integral part of the Polish Crown. Similar to the settlement with the Teutonic Order, the last Grand Master of Knights of the Sword received a territory as a hereditary duchy and a fief of Poland.

Ivan the Terrible responded to these events by launching a full-scale invasion. Sigismund was powerless to stop it. The Livonian War started in 1558, and the Russian army quickly took over the cities of Narva and Dorpat (today in Estonia). Several more towns and villages were conquered, but the Russians failed to take Riga, strategically the most important Livonian city. In 1563, Ivan the Terrible decided to switch his war tactics. Instead of fighting over Livonia, he attacked Lithuania directly. But other states had an interest in the area, particularly Denmark-Norway and Sweden, and the Russian tsar had to be wary of pushing Poland-Lithuania and the Scandinavian countries into an alliance.

The fighting continued for years, and Livonia ended up torn into pieces. The Polish-Lithuanian union controlled its south, while Russians held the center. The north was under the direct rule of the Swedish Crown. To all of them, Livonia was strategically important on the grand scale of their aspirations to control the Baltics. Danish and Swedish Crowns called their program of Baltic control *dominium maris baltici* and would engage in a series of conflicts known as the Northern Wars, which started with the Russo-Swedish War (1554-1557) and ended with the Great Northern War (1700-1721).

While the conflict in Lavonia and Lithuania was raging, Sigismund II Augustus became aware that he was the last Jagiellonian ruler in Poland. He married three times and had no male heir. Even the Polish-Lithuanian Parliament (called Sejm) agreed to accept any illegitimate son Sigismund II might have had with his mistresses, but the king remained unable to provide any children. The fact that he had no heir, along with Lithuania's inability to fight off the Russian invasion on its own, pushed the king to decide on a new type of union between Poland and Lithuania—one that would bring about a new polity and security to both sides. But he couldn't outright annex Lithuania without angering their nobility.

The cultural Polonization of Lithuania was already underway, and Lithuanian became the language of only the peasants. All the nobles and lesser lords spoke Polish, and all the official documents and records were written in Polish. But Polonizing Lithuania in a political sense was a different thing. It had to be done slowly, cautiously, and gradually. In 1565/66, the Sejm met in Vilnius and sanctioned the introduction of the Polish model of elective courts. The common law was codified (Second Lithuanian Statute), and the Lithuanian Sejm gained the same legislative powers as the Crown in Poland. All these changes helped engineer a new union from within.

The climax of the new Polish-Lithuanian union came in January of 1569 in Lublin. Sigismund announced that the Polish people and nobility were ready to accept a new and separate hierarchy of the Lithuanian state offices, under the condition that Sejm would become common, shared between Poland and Lithuania. The Polish people would also need to gain the right to acquire land and settle in the Grand Duchy. On March 1, the Lithuanian representatives walked out of the meeting, protesting the conditions the Crown was imposing on them. Sigismund was angry, and he immediately announced the annexation of parts of Lithuania's Rus territory. On March 16, he also announced that the separate status Royal Prussia enjoyed would come to an end. Prussian magnates didn't object. With the approval of the local nobles, in June 1569, the Crown annexed the palatinate of Kyiv.

All this was done to force the Lithuanians to accept a new union. Although it seemed that Sigismund would cave and annex Lithuania, he still believed that a willing union would be a better choice. The Poles finally agreed to offer Lithuanians reciprocal rights to buy land and settle in Poland, all to persuade them to comply with the union. On July 4, 1569, the king confirmed the new union as the Lithuanian nobles stopped protesting. A new political entity was created—the Kingdom of Poland and the Grand Duchy of Lithuania, unofficially known as the Polish-Lithuanian Commonwealth.

The new union of Poland and Lithuania was the greatest achievement of the last Jagiellonian king, Sigismund II Augustus. He imagined this new political entity based on the partnership of the nobles and the Crown. But the future would prove this was impossible to achieve, mainly because the nobles, land magnates, and the Crown worked only for their interests. The individualism Poland, Royal Prussia, and Lithuania fostered became particularly obvious after Sigismund's death. The new Sejm of 1570 and 1572 failed to develop new machinery for royal elections. Sigismund wanted to proclaim Ernest of Habsburg (youngest son of Holy Roman Emperor Maximilian II) as his successor. But the tyrannical Habsburg rule in Hungary and Bohemia resulted in a bad reputation among the Polish and Lithuanian nobles. When the king finally died on July 7, 1572, the nobles were left to choose the next monarch on their own.

Chapter 4 – The Polish-Lithuanian Commonwealth

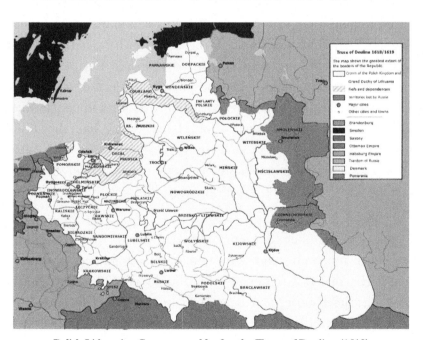

Polish-Lithuanian Commonwealth after the Truce of Deulino (1619)

On May 10, 1573, the Polish parliament elected Henry, Duke of Anjou, as the new monarch of the Polish-Lithuanian Commonwealth. But for him to accept the crown, he had to agree with the new constitutional ground rules concerning the elections of the Polish king. The Confederacy of Warsaw, an association created by the Polish parliament, drew up the new constitutional rule that the king would not proclaim a successor during his life. The Polish-Lithuanian Commonwealth was not hereditary, but an elective monarchy. Among other duties, the king was obliged to preserve interdenominational peace, consult the Sejm and the Senate on the issues of war and peace, and call the parliament every two years or whenever necessary. If the new king failed to observe the sworn commitments, he would lose the support of his subjects.

The Polish nobles chose the Duke of Anjou because France was willing to help them with the war with Russia and with the Ottoman Empire. In return, Poland would have a French ruler right on the border with Habsburg Austria, their rival in the European power struggle. The Lithuanian nobles boycotted the election of Henry of Anjou, but that didn't stop his coronation, as the Lithuanian ducal council confirmed his reign. But Henry didn't like the Polish political system. The French monarchic tradition was highly incompatible with the Polish political system in which all the nobles had the same rights and privileges regardless of their wealth and status.

But on September 13, Henry agreed to give up on the traditional hereditary monarchy and accept that Poland wanted to elect its kings. He signed a contract with the Polish-Lithuanian nation, known as the Henrician Articles, by which he officially recognized the constitutional law of the Commonwealth and its principles of government. He also had to sign *pacta conventa*, a contract with his subjects, which was always tailored to the specific king. Henry's *pacta conventa* regarded issues such as the grant of scholarships to the University of Sorbonne to the Polish-Lithuanian young nobles and promises of military and financial help in the war with Russia.

On June 18, 1574, Henry was in Wawel Castle in Krakow when he received the news that his brother, Charles IX of France, had died. Four days later, he left for France, leaving Poland in the hands of the Parliament. His absence started a constitutional crisis, as the parliamentarians started giving all educated and moderately wealthy men the right to engage in local governments. The Sejm then decided to petition the king to return to Wawel Castle. They sent Henry a message stating he would lose his Polish throne if he didn't return by May of 1575. Henry never returned, and the Sejm proclaimed the throne vacant. Although his reign in Poland was very short, he insisted on implementing some Polish cultural aspects in his French court. Among these were the use of forks, a septic tank outside the castle, and regulated hot and cold water in the bathrooms.

The Szlachta Power Grip

The social structure of the Polish-Lithuanian Union was already firmly in place by the time of the Union of Lublin (1569). The Polish-Lithuanian Commonwealth was settled in a system of estates that allowed certain social groups to enjoy wide measures of autonomy. Among them were the clergy, nobility, members of the wealthy bourgeoisie, and the Jews. They had the right to exercise jurisdiction over their members but only in matters that didn't concern other estates or the privileges of the Crown. Peasants were an estate on their own, but they lost many of the privileges they previously had and were under the direct control of the Crown, the nobility, or the church. A small group of free farmers existed but had little to no political influence.

The Polish social estates were not what we imagine social classes to be. They never depended on individual or collective wealth, the economic position of their members, or their productive role in the kingdom. Estates were separated exclusively along the lines of their legal rights and privileges. Economic differences certainly existed, but they never influenced the intended functions of one group within the society. For example, a nobleman could be landless and poor, no wealthier than his peasant neighbors. But unlike his neighbors, he enjoyed fiscal, legal, and political privileges that came with his noble status. In the same manner, a wealthy Jewish family was restricted in its social and political role simply because of its religious choice. Jews would be allowed to join the ranks of the bourgeois or nobility only if they converted to Christianity.

People were born into their social estates, which made their ranks hereditary. Mobility between different estates was very hard. Economic well-being meant little because of the strict legal framework that was put in place. One could not move up the social estate ladder simply by acquiring more land or money. To develop the socio-economic classes that are familiar to us today, Poland needed to deconstruct its tradition of hereditary social estates. But that came much later. The fifteenth, sixteenth, and seventeenth centuries were a period in which the system of social estates flourished.

In the history of Poland, the most recent estate to emerge was the Szlachta (nobility). Their origin is unknown, although each noble family came up with legends and stories that connected them to the ancient past of Poland. By the 16th century, they became a superior estate that exercised control over all Polish-Lithuanian institutions and perfected the laws that would give them even more power in the subsequent period. The Szlachta had a dominant role in the political, social, and cultural life of the Polish-Lithuanian Union and Commonwealth, enabling them to organize the state to suit their own interests. Poland-Lithuania was a piece of heaven on earth for the nobility, but that also made it a hell for peasants.

The Szlachta emerged as an estate with tremendous political and social influence because their path was paved by the kings of the 14th century. Many Polish kings granted various immunities to individual knights and lords, but in the 14th century, the practice expanded to the nobility as a community, not as individuals. For example, anxious to secure the succession of his daughter Jadwiga, Louis of Anjou (who reigned in Poland from 1370-1382) exempted the nobles from paying land tax. That is how the estate of the nobility was first established. Soon, the Szlachta had very high bargaining power they could use in times of crisis or succession to the Polish throne.

The Lithuanian boyars received the same rights and privileges as the Polish Szlachta in 1413, with the renewed Union of Poland and Lithuania signed in Horodlo. In 1496, the nobles were given the right to monopolize the land holding. On June 14, 1505, the Sejm issued a new constitution known as *Nihil novi nisi commune consensu* (Nothing new without the common consent). This meant that no new laws would be implemented without parliament's approval, whose members were strictly chosen from the ranks of the nobility. Thus, the concept of "Noble Democracy" was born. The Szlachta used their newly-gained legislative supremacy to acquire more advantages over the rest of Polish-Lithuanian society.

The Szlachta easily gained a monopoly over not only the land property but also the government, administration, and central political life of Poland-Lithuania. The rights of the clergy, bourgeois, and peasantry were restricted. That meant that all the high positions within the church were reserved for members of the nobility, and all the burghers, except within Royal Prussia, were required to sell their land properties to the nobility. Peasants were not allowed to settle in towns; they could only move from one village to another. Even the small freedom of movement peasants still had was crushed with the new legislation in 1518, when they were strictly tied to the land and the landowner's will. The only obligation the nobility had to keep their privileges was to provide unpaid military service.

The Polish-Lithuanian Commonwealth's nobility was extremely numerous by the European standards of the time. They numbered 25,000 noble families and around 500,000 individuals. They represented 6.6 percent of the total population of the Commonwealth's 7.5 million people. In the 17th century, the number rose to 9 percent and continued to rise throughout the 18th century. The Polish-Lithuanian Commonwealth had the highest percentage of nobility among European countries. It was followed by Spain and Hungary, whose nobility totaled around 5 percent of their population. France and England were contrasting central European kingdoms, with only 1 to 2 percent.

The formal privileges the Szlachta acquired gave them protection from the king's political ambitions but, at the same time, protected them from modernizing their state. Their prosperity was guaranteed by massive legislation they perfected for two centuries. The nobility was a close-knit estate that created their own reality—and also the reality of all other social estates of Poland. Their obligations to the state were minimal, which meant they fully gained what they called a "Golden Liberty." They controlled the legislature and the election of the king, and no future Polish monarch could hope to break away from the powerful grip of the Szlachta.

The closeness of the Szlachta estate was demonstrated by the new legislation adopted by the Sejm in 1578 and 1601. The first limited the king's power to create knighthood except in case of wartime or during a parliament session. The second altogether banned monarchs from knighting people without the strict approval of the Sejm. Peasants could rise in their social ranks only with the approval of their lords. In 1641, the parliament approved the extension of Polish-Lithuanian nobility to foreign nobles, and in 1775, they made land ownership a prior condition for everyone who wanted to enter the Szlachta estate.

The Polish nobility was extreme in their high regard for "blue blood," which could be compared to racism. Many nobles from outside even criticized Poland for the extreme protection the Szlachta enjoyed—or rather, the lack of protection for all other social estates. A death sentence was Szlachta's answer to many crimes performed by peasants, and the sentence could be executed by any nobleman. Dungeons were a common part of the household, and chains, torture devices, and weapons were common household items. The Burghers and the peasants had no access to education, and by law, their lives and property were less worthy than those of the nobles. But within the nobility, the equality of sexes was always practiced; women had the same rights and privileges as men and could own properties.

Báthory - The Transylvanian Ruler

Royal elections were held in 1576, and Anna Jagiellon was chosen as the new Queen of the Polish-Lithuanian Commonwealth. She was the sister of Sigismund II Augustus, the last Jagiellonian king, and the only choice that would keep the dynastic line uninterrupted. Anna didn't marry until she was fifty-two years old, though she didn't lack suitors. Finally, she was engaged to Stephen Báthory, Voivode of Transylvania, as the Polish parliamentarians chose him as her co-ruler. Once again, the Lithuanian representatives didn't engage in voting but recognized the couple after their coronation on May 1,1576.

Stephen Báthory proved to be admirably qualified to take the position of a monarch. He never sought the position for himself. He was approached by Polish representatives who wanted him as their king. The motivation of these representatives was to undermine the Habsburg pretensions to the Polish throne and install anyone but a Habsburg. Among other qualifications, Stephen was already a proven defender of the Christian faith, and that was his advantage over the other nominees. He fought for the independence of his native Transylvania, was wounded and imprisoned, and managed to be elected Voivod of Transylvania despite the hostility of Holy Roman Emperor Maximilian II (1564-

1576). He was Catholic, but all religions enjoyed autonomy in his domain of Transylvania. He had a good education and started his career at the court of Vienna, from where he later embarked on a tour of Western Europe to familiarize himself with different courts and policies.

The officials of the city of Danzig supported the Habsburgs for the Polish throne, and once Stephen was crowned, he and Anna had to make an example of the city and discipline its officials. In September 1576, King Stephen announced a commercial blockade of the city. All Polish trade was therefore transferred to Elbląg. But Danzig continued to resist Báthory's rule, and its citizens burned the Abbey of Oliwa. As a reprisal, Stephen and Anna sent an army to appease the city. Although the Polish royal army killed most of the opponents, they were unable to take the city. The peace negotiations started at Malbork Castle on April 17, 1577, and a new relationship between Danzig and Poland had to be established, although it would not be fully drafted and agreed upon until 1585.

After dealing with Danzig, Stephen Báthory started a judicial reform of the Polish-Lithuanian Commonwealth. He raised Jan Zamoyski, Deputy Chancellor and Polish nobleman, to the position of Crown Chancellor. Then, he tasked Zamoyski with developing a new judicial system that would put all affairs directly under the nobility's control. Thus King Stephen gave up the Crown's prerogative to hear appeals in all civil and criminal cases. In 1578, the Polish Sejm founded the Crown Tribunal, and in 1581, a similar institution in Lithuania. These tribunals aimed to prevent royal tyranny and ensure that the Sejm and the Crown worked closely, even in matters of purely royal interest.

The next reform concerned the army. Stephen Báthory persuaded the Polish parliament to approve the formation of the *piechota wybraniecka* (selected infantry). All Crown estates were to send soldiers to serve in this new regiment at a rate of one soldier per every twenty holdings. The remaining nineteen families that didn't send any of their members to serve would support that one soldier. The *piechota wybraniecka* were armed with muskets, but they proved inefficient in fighting due to their lack of training and other military equipment. They were discontinued in the early 18th century.

The old *jazda kopijnicza* (mounted spearmen) were replaced with the famous "Winged Hussars," the legendary formation of many European battlefields of the 16th and 17th centuries. Hussars served in the Polish army much earlier, but only as Serbo-Hungarian mercenaries. It was Stephen Báthory who introduced them as a regular regiment and started recruiting from Polish estates for their ranks. In the Polish army, the Hussars became an elite cavalry unit, and most of their recruits came from the Szlachta. Their main weapon was the long lance, which made them a heavy cavalry, but they were also equipped with daggers and sabers, and later even pistols. But they are most famous for the large wings that adorned their backs. Scholars still debate if these wings were attached to the rider's back or the back of the saddle. They were heavy, and their only purpose was to intimidate the opponent with their appearance and the rattling noise they made. It seems unlikely a soldier would be maneuverable enough on a horse with such a burden on his back, so most scholars believe that the wings were attached to the saddle. Whatever the case, the wings gave the Polish Hussars the nickname "The Angels of Death." In 1578, the Dnieper Cossacks, who lived in the old Tartar style, approached King Stephen and asked to join the Polish military. A new regiment was thus created of Cossack volunteers who, in return for their services, received the same annual pay as the hussars.

The purpose of the Polish army reform was the concern a new king had regarding his eastern neighbor, the Grand Duchy of Moscow, and its ruler, Ivan IV ("the Terrible"). When he accepted the Polish Crown, Stephen Báthory inherited the earlier conflict between Lithuania and the Muscovites. Báthory's main concern wasn't this particular conflict but Ivan's tendency to acquire more land, his brutality, and his imperialistic aspirations. The Polish-Lithuanian Commonwealth was Ivan's final objective, and for Stephen, the fight against the Muscovites was a fight for the survival of his kingdom. With a reformed army and his new Royal Chancellor and main adviser, Zamoyski, Stephen Báthory defeated Russian forces in Livonia and took Polotsk (1579) and Velikiye Luki (1580).

In 1581, Stephen even managed to lead his army into Russian territory and besiege the city of Pskov. He was unable to take the city, but he cut its supply line for over five months and held the city in blockade until the end of the war. During the truce negotiations, Ivan IV ceded most of the Livonian territory, together with Polatsk and Veliz. In return, the Commonwealth gave up its control of Velikiye Luki and Nevel. The Livonian War officially ended with the Truce of Yam-Zapolsky, signed on January 15, 1582. The siege of Pskov thus ended with neither side managing to break it. The Polish army celebrated the end of the war as a victory.

With the end of the Livonian War, King Stephen Báthory started planning grand alliances between the Russian Empire, Poland, and other great European kingdoms. In 1583, he approached Ivan IV with the idea of a common crusade against Crimea. In 1584, he dreamed of an expedition to Constantinople, but the death of Ivan the Terrible prevented him from acting further. He also planned a grand federation of Poland, Lithuania, Muscovy, and Hungary, but the Sejm declined such a proposal. Stephen Báthory fell into a deep depression and started accusing the Poles of ingratitude. He composed his will in 1585, although there were no signs he could soon die. In it, he favored his native Transylvania and continued to belittle the Polish Sejm and Szlachta, accusing them of not seeing the grand picture. In 1586, Stephen died suddenly, suffering no illness prior. This prompted rumors of poisoning, though no evidence was ever confirmed to support this.

Vasa - The Swedish Connection

In the elections of 1587, the Polish Crown was won by Sigismund III of the Swedish Vasa dynasty. Sigismund was a son of Catherine Jagiellon, daughter of late King Sigismund I of Poland. However, that wasn't the only reason he was elected to the Polish throne. At the time, Sweden was very similar to the Polish-Lithuanian Republic: it was a dual state made of Sweden and Finland, and its society was dominated by powerful noble houses. Since power was in the hands of the nobility, the Swedish monarchy was as weak as the Polish monarchy. The Polish nobles gave an advantage to the throne pretender, who could easily understand that they were in charge. The Polish nobles also liked the idea of a foreign king who would be more concerned with the politics of his homeland, Sweden, and would leave Poland's politics to the parliament.

Sigismund was also the favorite candidate of Chancellor Zamoyski, who was ready for the conflict with the Habsburgs that was certain to break out if their candidate lost. The Austrians attacked Krakow, but the Polish army was ready to repel them. On December 27, Sigismund was crowned King of Poland, and although the Habsburgs had the pope's backing, they could do nothing but watch.

Although Zamoyski's campaign for Sigismund was successful, he would later regret it. Sigismund wanted to abdicate in 1588 when he had to sign the Third Lithuanian Statute, but instead, he sought to sell his Polish crown to the Habsburgs. In 1589, he had already announced he would depart Poland and return to Sweden, but the Swedish nobility made it clear they didn't want him. Nevertheless, after his father's death, John III, Sigismund sought to acquire the Swedish Crown and went to Stockholm. But only after ten years of succession crisis were the Swedes willing to crown him their king. Even after becoming the king, Sigismund was resented by the

Swedish nobles. After five months of constant quarrels, he had to flee the country. In 1599, the Swedes formally deposed him.

Sigismund's struggles in Sweden turned many Polish nobles against him. If nothing else, they expected their king to at least maintain the image of concern for Poland. Sigismund did nothing of the sort, and his reputation suffered. Chancellor Zamoyski proved to be a competent leader of the Polish-Lithuanian Republic, but he was not innovative, and he made no progress in developing the constitution. The king's power was still very limited, and the nobles continued expanding their privileges. Zamoyski also failed to address the problem of royal succession and limited it to several named candidates. Nevertheless, he led Poland in its Golden Age with the expansion of Baltic trade and control of Danzig, the richest Baltic port. The prestige, power, and economic influence of the Polish-Lithuanian Republic reached its peak during the reign of Sigismund III, though not thanks to him.

But Sigismund III remained influential in the sphere of foreign policy. He managed to turn the Polish-Lithuanian Republic in a direction that could have been avoided. He continued to pursue his claim to the Swedish throne until 1660, resulting in a war with Sweden that lasted for the next thirty years. In fact, the conflict between Poland and Sweden extended to the Thirty Years' War once Swedish King Gustavus Adolphus decided to join the German side of the war and occupied Prussia, though he never managed to control Danzig.

Sigismund also sought to expand Polish territory and revived the old war with the Muscovy. Sweden joined this war, too, but it never made an alliance with Poland or Muscovy and only sought its own interests. The last war between Poland and Sweden occurred during the reign of Charles X, nephew of Gustavus Adolphus, who decided to attack the Polish-Lithuanian Republic. By then, Poland was ruled by Sigismund's son Władysław IV Vasa (1632-1648). The Swedish king was reluctant to allow the Muscovites to take any of the

Republic's territory, and he fought them off. He didn't do it to help Poland but to take the territory for Sweden. His actions resulted in confusion and destruction that shook Poland for the next six years, a period known as *Potop*, or "the Deluge." Various foreign invaders could easily pray on Polish-Lithuanian territory. The Swedes easily took over the Grand Duchy of Lithuania, Greater Poland, Warsaw, and Krakow. Polish King John II Casimir Vasa (1648–1668) was forced to seek protection in Silesia while his army abandoned him and entered Swedish service.

Even though the Polish army had abandoned King John II Casimir Vasa, one military commander remained loyal: Stefan Czarniecki. He was a petty nobleman who distinguished himself during the Deluge and became a Polish national hero, celebrated even today in the national anthem. It was he who started turning the tide of the war against Sweden. He successfully drove them out of Warsaw and persuaded their Prussian allies to defect. In 1658, Czarniecki led the attack on Sweden from Danish Jutland, as he had joined the Danish-Swedish War. When the Peace of Oliwa was concluded in 1660, Czarniecki was transferred to the Russian front, where he continued to distinguish himself. He was rewarded with the title Voivode of Kyiv and continued to serve the Polish Crown until he died in 1665.

The Peace of Oliwa ended the Polish-Swedish struggle, but it was Sweden that got control over Livonia, with Poland controlling only Semigallia and the Duchy of Courland. But Poland managed to leave the conflict, and the Polish-Lithuanian Republic was revived while Sweden continued to fight the Muscovy. The conflict with Sweden was never bipolar. Muscovy was always involved, as the entire conflict was a power struggle over control of the Baltics. The final conflict between Poland and Muscovy was fought between 1700 and 1721 in what is known as the Great Northern War.

John III Sobieski

John III Sobieski at the Battle of Vienna in 1683
by Martino Altomonte)
https://en.wikipedia.org/wiki/John_III_Sobieski#/media/File:Altomonte_Battle_of_Vienna.jpg

John II Casimir Vasa abdicated the throne in 1668, after the death of his wife. He retreated to France, where he became an abbot of a Parisian monastery. His abdication left the Polish throne vacant, and another election was needed. The Polish nobility chose Michał Korybut as their candidate. He was the son of a very powerful magnate from the borderlands of Eastern Poland, and the nobility regarded him as a young, inexperienced prince who would be easy to manipulate. On September 29, 1669, Michał started his reign after winning the majority of the votes of the nobles, who wished to finally have a native ruler instead of a foreigner.

The reign of Michał I lasted for only four years, most of which were spent fighting internal struggles, as an anti-royalist faction rose and was determined to bring a French candidate to the throne. During his reign, Poland also lost control over all of its Ukrainian territories, which were now under Turkish rule. During these events, King Michał showed no effort to take control over his magnates and the army or lead the war against the Turks. He died in his prime at age thirty-three, probably of food poisoning—though the possibility of murder was never dismissed.

John III Sobieski won the next elections and ruled from 1674 to 1696. He became a leading figure in the Polish-Lithuanian Commonwealth due to his military successes in the Russo-Polish War, the Deluge, and the conflicts with the Ottoman Empire. Just one day after the death of Michał I, Sobieski won a great victory against the Turks at Chocim on the Dniester. When he entered Warsaw three months later, he already had the support of most of the noblemen, and he won the elections with virtually no opposition. He was one of the rare Polish monarchs to have such wide military experience before claiming the throne. Sobieski was also the only Polish ruler whose fame went beyond the country's borders. He was an avid fighter against the Ottoman Empire and was celebrated by many nations for his war achievements against the Turks.

To the nobles of Danzig or western Poland in general, the new king seemed obsessed with the Ottomans. But understanding his origins can easily explain this. He was from the eastern borderlands, where trouble with the Ottomans was a constant. Although Sobieski received his education at the Jagiellonian University in Krakow, his eastern upbringing made him choose a military career while still in his youth. His natural inclination toward the military influenced his reign, and it is no wonder he started military reform as early as possible in his reign. All the reforms he made were in support of his favorite regiment, the Winged Hussars, that had brought him so many victories. Therefore, he reduced the number of pikemen and increased the cavalry. Cossack regiments were given chain mail armor and short lances for greater mobility. Most importantly, Sobieski increased the army from 18,000 to 54,000 men.

The coronation ceremony of John III Sobieski was frequently postponed, as the king was mostly absent from Warsaw. But unlike his predecessors, who were foreigners and absent because they preferred their native countries, Sobieski spent most of his time on the battlefield. In 1674-5, he was actively involved in breaking the Turkish siege of Lviv. In 1676, his Polish army was exhausted and locked in its camp at Żurawno (Zhuravno). However, the Turkish force under the command of Ibrahim Szejtan was unable to break the Polish resistance. The Battle of Żurawno was fought between September 25 and October 14, and the losses were heavy on both sides. Poles showed no intention to stop fighting, and Ibrahim Szejtan was forced to initiate peace negotiations. The Treaty of Żurawno was signed in favor of the Polish-Lithuanian Commonwealth, ending its obligation to pay tribute to the Ottoman Empire.

But the peace didn't last long. In 1683, the Great Turkish War began, which lasted until 1699. Sobieski swiftly signed an agreement of mutual assistance with the ambassador of the Holy Roman Empire. When Emperor Leopold II called for help against the Ottomans, Sobieski was ready. The Ottomans sent their army from Belgrade, the shortest route to Vienna, to besiege the city. Sobieski received around 1,200,000 ducats to send a relief army to Vienna and break the siege. The Holy Roman Empire even offered him the position of commander-in-chief of all allied forces if he came to the battlefield personally.

The Ottoman army was quick: it laid siege to Vienna in the middle of July with its 140,000 soldiers. The allies who were supposed to come help the Holy Roman Empire were slow. Sobieski had only started gathering his forces in Krakow in the middle of summer, and he had yet to cross the Carpathians in the autumn. Sobieski commanded over 74,000 men, a combined Polish, Lithuanian, and German army. His army would meet the enemy on the battlefield on September 12, and it was a great victory for the allies.

There are different accounts of the battle, and the responsibility for the victory was given to different individuals and armies throughout history. The Germans focus on the success of Charles of Lorraine, who led his army on the left wing and broke the Turkish force at Kahlenberg. The Polish stressed the importance of their artillery that dispersed the Turkish counterattack in the middle. Sobieski personally led his Winged Hussars in a spectacular charge on the right flank. He ordered the Hussars to charge on the main tent of the grand vizier. Sobieski was on his horse, right in the middle of his cavalry. By the following night, he used the vizier's tent as his personal headquarters. The victory was certain, and the next day, the Polish king joined the army in pursuing the fleeing Ottomans.

In 1684, following the victory at Vienna, Sobieski decided to fully commit himself to the efforts of the Holy League, which comprised the Holy Roman Empire, Venice, Russia, and the Polish-Lithuanian Commonwealth. But seventeen years of uninterrupted campaigning would cost him greatly. The Commonwealth army was exhausted, and so were its finances. Any intention the king or the Sejm had to launch internal reforms had to be postponed. The Commonwealth also abandoned its previous plans to regain all of Prussia and continue the conflict with Muscovy revolving around their Ukrainian territories. Because of the abandonment of these plans, Ukraine was assigned to Muscovy, which then transformed into Russia. The existence of such a great Russia tipped the power balance scales of Europe. Poland gained nothing by joining the Holy League, and even Prussia would soon declare itself a kingdom. Only Russia and Austria emerged from the Great Turkish War as great powers. The Polish-Lithuanian Commonwealth was seen as an invalid state, and the prospect of its partitioning became very real.

After such failures, the king decided to immerse himself in private business. He had no real domestic power since the nobles continued to make all major decisions, so he concentrated his efforts on securing the succession of his son, Jakub. To secure the elections for his son, Sobieski had to secure a good marriage, but this proved to be difficult. Jakub's fiancé Ludwika Karolina Radziwiłł decided to marry the prince of Prussia. He then negotiated a marriage with a Transylvanian princess, but the Habsburgs were offended by this and started threatening Poland. Sobieski had no other choice but to opt for a Habsburg bride. But the nobles would not have it, and Jakub's royal succession misfired. In June of 1696, John III Sobieski died of a heart attack.

Chapter 5 – A Path to Destruction

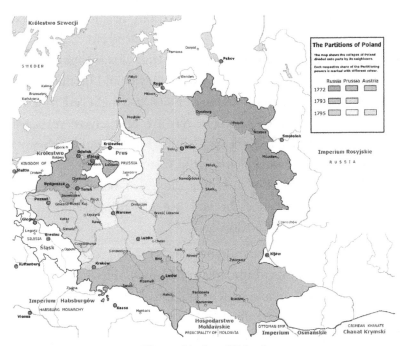

The partitioning of Poland
Halibutt, CC-BY-SA-3.0;
https://en.wikipedia.org/wiki/Partitions_of_Poland#/media/File:Rzeczpospolita_Rozbiory_3.png

After the reign of John III Sobieski, a period of humiliation for Poland began. For the next sixty years, Poland was subjected to foreign rule. The Saxon noble house of Wettin managed to succeed to the Polish throne against all odds. Jakub Sobieski, the son of the previous ruler, was forced to retreat from the elections of 1697. The French candidate, Prince de Conti, was the favorite of the majority, but he was unable to secure his victory in the end. The Saxon candidate, Friedrich-August, came to the elections at the last minute and immediately started bribing, threatening, and manipulating the Polish nobles. When he finally promised to convert to Catholicism, the Bishop of Kujawy (now Diocese of Włocławek) simply declared him elected. In September, the elector of Saxon was crowned Augustus II of Poland (r. 1697-1706/1709-1733).

In the beginning, the Polish-Lithuanian Commonwealth and Saxony union had many benefits for both partners. They could jointly fight off the threat of Prussian, Russian, and Swedish territorial ambitions. Since Poland-Lithuania was a larger partner in this union, the Polish nobles presumed they would be the dominant force behind the decision-making. They also believed they could maintain separate interests from Saxony and enjoy yet another absent ruler who would rather spend time in his native Saxony and deal with its native issues, leaving the Commonwealth in the hands of the nobility. The Polish-Lithuanians also believed they could manipulate the Saxon elector and use his influence in the Holy Roman Empire to their advantage.

The private interests of Augustus II often clashed with the interests of the Polish-Lithuanian Republic. He had a personal alliance with Russia, and when the Great Northern War (1700-1721) started, he joined the fight but didn't involve the Republic. However, Poland-Lithuania would become one of the greatest victims of this war it never intended to fight. When Charles XII of Sweden defeated Augustus's Saxon forces at Riga, he continued marching south. Soon, the Duchy of Courland, a territory belonging to the Commonwealth, was occupied. In 1702, the Swedish army crossed the Polish-Lithuanian Republic from north to south and took the cities of Wilno, Warsaw, and Krakow.

The Swedes organized a Confederation of Warsaw and put forward their claimant to the Polish-Lithuanian throne, a nobleman from Greater Poland, Stanisław Leszczyński (r. 1704-1709). The city of Sandomierz remained pro-Saxon but had to rely on Russian help. Augustus retreated to Lviv before trying to retake Warsaw in 1706. But the Swedish king Charles XII wanted to deal with Augustus once and for all, and he marched his army into the heartland of Saxony. Suffering defeat, Augustus II had to sign the Treaty of Altranstädt, renouncing the Polish throne. But soon, the Confederation of Sandomierz, aided by the Russians, managed to defeat the Swedish army at Kalisz. The Swedes departed for Russia, as it became clear they could not secure the victory by a proxy war in Poland. The Republic was left in the hands of a new king, but he soon lost his position when the Swedes suffered a great defeat against Russia in the Battle of Poltava in 1709. The next year, Augustus II returned to the Polish throne, and the union with Saxony was restored.

But these events represented only the first stage of the Great Northern War, and the Polish-Lithuanian Commonwealth would continue to suffer. Anti-Saxon sentiment rose, and in 1715, the Polish nobles formed the General Confederation of Tarnogrod, intending to expel Saxon rule from the Republic. Throughout 1715 and 1716, it looked as if the confederation would succeed, as they managed to push Augustus back to Saxony. But the arrival of the Russian army shocked them. The Russian tsar, Peter the Great (r. 1682-1725), considered Saxony and Poland his client states, and he was annoyed by their squabbling. He was determined to make them work together and offered himself to be an arbiter in the negotiations. But his plan behind this offer was to seize control over all Polish affairs.

The negotiations were held in 1716 in Warsaw, and Augustus II agreed to remove his Saxon army from the Polish-Lithuanian territory. The Russian tsar became the guarantee of the agreement between the king and the nobles in the form of a written constitution. This also gave him the power to interfere in the internal affairs of Poland, and there was nothing the Polish could do against the encroachments of the Russians. The Sejm even swore to accept the agreement and the constitution without any protest. This is why this parliamentary session is known as the Silent Sejm in Polish history. Surrounded by Russian soldiers, the nobles signed the agreement and gave away Polish freedom.

Thus the Polish-Lithuanian Commonwealth entered modern history with Russian supremacy looming over it. The Commonwealth became a Russian protectorate, but the state remained autonomous for most of the 18th century. Russia would then start to incorporate Polish and Lithuanian territories into its empire. Russia wasn't alone in this, as Austria, Prussia, and Germany also took part in the partitioning of Poland. But although Austrians and Germans would come and go, Russians were there to stay. The political scene of Poland became a mirror image of the one in Russia, and the country's interests came second to the Polish nobility. The Polish army was extremely reduced and its finances cut off, while neighboring countries started massive militarization. Poland had no chance of defending itself from preying neighbor states.

King Augustus II died in 1733, and yet another election in Poland led to an international war. In September 1733, a French candidate, Stanisław Leszczyński, won the Crown in the elections, but Austria and Russia supported another Wettin successor. The War of the Polish Succession was fought for the next two years, but most of the battles were fought outside of Poland. Renewed elections were held in October 1733. Under the pressure of Russian bayonets, the Polish elected Saxon successor, Augustus III (r. 1733-

1763). Although the war continued after the election of Augustus III (it officially ended with the Treaty of Vienna 1738), general relief could be felt. The union of Saxony-Poland-Lithuania continued, and for the next thirty years, the reign of Augustus III would pass with little to no disturbances.

The new king had no real power, and it seems he was satisfied with this, as he wanted to take no part in decision-making. The Russians had a major influence on every sphere of life in 18th century Poland. During the War of Austrian Succession (1742-1748) and the Seven Years War (1756-1763), Augustus III was concerned only with the well-being of his native Saxony. The Russian army was free to cross Polish territory as they transported their troops to Prussia and Pomerania, where the battlefield was. During this time, the centralized power of the Polish-Lithuanian Republic was destroyed. The Sejm didn't exist anymore, and all their work was passed down to local rulers. The whole country was divided into a myriad of small private estates, where local magnates ruled as emperors, often with direct Russian or French support.

The cities and towns of the Polish-Lithuanian Commonwealth shrank, and all the bourgeois left the country. Poverty rose as the economy stagnated, but the nobility and the magnates continued enjoying their private wealth. Their patronage greatly contributed to the culture. Architecture, music, and theater were superb, and the culture and arts were on the rise. But some magnates were well aware of the real condition of the republic—of the poverty that the majority of people suffered under the gleaming surface of the Warsaw balls. These magnates tried to improve the economy of Poland and Lithuania by opening factories, abolishing serfdoms on their private estates, opening public schools and libraries, and developing mining and metallurgy industries. But all this was done for nothing, as in 1795, the Russian army plundered the achievements of the magnates and took most of the accumulated technologies, products, and resources to Russia.

The Partitioning

When Augustus III died, Saxon rule came to an end, as Catherine the Great (r. 1762-1796) of Russia had different plans for the Polish-Lithuanian Commonwealth. She installed her confidant, a Polish noble named Stanislaw-August Poniatowski (r.1764-1795), on the Polish throne. He was to be the last king of the Commonwealth, ruling through the death throes of his country and silently watching all three stages of its partitioning in 1773, 1793, and 1795. The partitioning itself was without precedent in modern European history. It was the first and last time the great powers tore apart a historical state in cold blood. The European sentiment at the time was that somehow Poland deserved annihilation, but no one knew exactly why. Many tried to answer that question by stating how the Commonwealth was constantly in a state of anarchy and that, as such, it didn't deserve to be a part of the modern European world.

Although not exactly in anarchy, the Poland-Lithuanian Republic at the time was not far from it. Still a dual state, its politicians had to deal with the conflicting interests of both parties. After the Silent Sejm of 1717, its leaders were unable to repair any grievances and weaknesses the state suffered. All attempts at reform failed due to the different goals of the Kingdom of Poland and the Grand Duchy of Lithuania. The monarchy existed, and the king was elected, but he had no real power and represented nothing more than a point of interest for international diplomacy. The Golden Freedom the nobles of Poland-Lithuania had enjoyed for generations, which they saw as the pinnacle of the Republic, now meant nothing as the Sejm stopped gathering.

It didn't help that neighboring countries promoted the internal struggles of Poland. Russia was constantly interfering in its internal affairs, and Austria, Prussia, Germany, Sweden, and France used Poland to settle their personal quarrels. Whenever the Polish nobles tried to change their country for the better, they were countered by Russian and Prussian efforts to keep them in perpetual disorder. Polish-Lithuanians had no desire to wallow in anarchy, but their desperate efforts to escape it only contributed to the grave state of the Republic. When the Sejm finally met in 1764 and tried to centralize the state's finances, the Prussian army moved to the Vistula river, from where they could continuously bombard and terrorize Polish shipping until the matter was dropped. The Russians continued sending their army to supervise the elections, guaranteeing the victory for the candidate of their choosing.

Russia intended to annex Poland, but the matter was constantly postponed because there were two groups within Russia advocating a different approach. The military group was straightforward, demanding total and immediate annexation. The politicians were more careful and wanted to continue playing the role of Polish protector, promising safety and investments. Poland would be Russia's advance post in Europe, a vassal state whose loyalty could easily be maintained by empty promises. This was a favorite approach of politicians because it was inexpensive, and Catherine the Great at first shared this view. But later in her reign, she would have enough of such games and discard this approach in favor of direct annexation.

Prussia's role and view of the Polish-Lithuanian Republic were somewhat different. Unlike Russia, Prussia was a small state and couldn't easily afford prolonged wars, although its territorial ambitions were insatiable. Before the partitioning of Poland, Prussia was in a twenty-year-long conflict with Russia, and it lost Silesia in 1740. They were spared destruction only because Elizabeth I of Russia (r. 1741-1762) died and Peter III was proclaimed emperor. Peter III admired Prussian king Frederick II the Great (1740-1786) and decided to stop Russia's participation in the Seven Years' War. Russia and Prussia signed a peace treaty by which the two countries became allies instead of enemies. Prussia was finally able to exercise its expansion tendencies, and Poland was there for grabs.

Austria was exhausted by the Seven Years' War and had no plans to expand. The Habsburgs were enemies of Prussia, and they feared Russia. They were very unlikely to participate in the partitioning of Poland, especially because they still remembered how Sobieski broke the siege of Vienna, and their sentiment towards the Republic was positive. But in the end, Austria couldn't resist its imperialism, and it too took part in the partitioning.

All three states used Polish anarchy as the excuse for the partitioning, although their territorial ambitions were the real reason behind it. When the Polish organized the Bar Confederation in 1768 to overthrow the Russian influence, it only provoked the great powers and justified their invasion of Poland-Lithuania. Frederick II of Prussia went even further and accused Poland of being so weak that it threatened international security, especially after Austria joined the Ottoman Empire in an alliance against Russia. To prevent the arbitrary annexations, Frederick called for immediate and legal partitioning of Poland. In 1772, Maria Theresa, Queen-Empress of Austria, accepted the Prussian invitation to join the partitioning.

Russian, Prussian, and Austrian diplomats spent the next five months settling the details. In the end, Prussia gained Royal Prussia, Chelmno, and Kujawy. Frederick II refused control of Danzig to show his modesty. Russia took Polish Livonia, Homel, Mscislaw, Vitebsk, and Polotsk. Austria gained the most with a large part of Lesser Poland that housed approximately 2,130,000 people, though territorially it only grabbed 11.8 percent. Russia gained the largest part at 12.7 percent of Poland and 1,300,000 people, while Prussia gained only 5 percent and 580,000 people. The treaty of partition was signed on August 5, 1772, in St. Petersburg.

The first partitioning of Poland had a second partitioning as an eventual consequence, and the second had a third: nothing can come out of violence except more violence. The first partitioning only provoked the tensions that were supposed to be resolved by the act itself. The entire partitioning scenario came about again in the periods between 1773 and 1793 and again in 1794-1795. Polish people continued trying to reform what was left of their state, and for that, they were punished. In 1792, a Polish-Russian War broke out because the Polish-Lithuanian Commonwealth, with the assistance of Prussia, brought forth a new constitution. Catherine the Great was furious, as she feared Russian influence in Poland would be diminished. The war ended with Polish capitulation and the annulment of the constitution. Prussia and Russia made a new deal and grabbed more of Poland's territory. Russia receiving Kyiv, Minsk, Podole, Braclaw, and parts of Vilnius, Nowogródek, Brest-Litovsk, and Volhynian Voivodeship. Prussia took Gdansk and Torun, Poznan, Gniezno, Krakow, Masovia, Sieradz, and many more voivodships that became southern Prussia.

In 1794, the Poles, dissatisfied with their capitulation in the Polish-Russian War, started an uprising known as the Kościuszko Uprising, bearing the name of its leader. The people fought with the hope they would get rid of foreign influence, if not return some of the territories taken from them. But although the Poles had some initial success, they didn't have the manpower or the military equipment to fight the stronger Russians. The uprising failed. The result was the third partitioning in which Austria, Russia, and Prussia once again divided the territories of the Polish-Lithuanian Commonwealth among themselves. Austria gained southern Masovia and western Galicia, Prussia took the rest of Masovia, Warsaw, and Podlachia, and Russia gained all the remaining territories of eastern Lithuania.

The Poland-Lithuanian Commonwealth was effectively dissolved, and Poland would not exist for the next 123 years. The death of Poland received no attention from the rest of Europe, whose eyes were fixed on the events in France. At the time of the partitioning of Poland, French revolutionary armies started advancing into Spanish Galicia, Piedmont, and Catalonia; Holland,

Belgium, and Rhineland had already been taken. Foreign diplomats in Warsaw left the country, not even waiting to see the destiny of the country in which they once served. The death of Poland was a silent event.

Chapter 6 – Poland in Pieces

A scene of Warsaw at the beginning of the November Uprising of 1830
https://en.wikipedia.org/wiki/History_of_Poland#/media/File:Marcin_Zaleski,_Wzi%C4%
99cie_Arsena%C5%82u.jpg

Between 1795 and 1918, Poland remained politically and territorially divided and under foreign rule. Amazingly, through times of constant struggle for independence, Polish culture and its traditions, as well as the traditional values of the nobility, remained untouched. Even under Protestant Prussia and Orthodox Russia, Poland remained loyal to its Roman Catholicism. But varying development of the economy, politics, and society was inevitable as different parts of Poland came under the direct influence of their foreign rulers. Regional differences became even more prominent, and exclusive ethnic and linguistic nationalism developed. These different nationalisms would later make the issue of the national identity of Poland a very complex question.

After the third partitioning, the Polish nation had to deal with its survival. The convention signed by Austria, Prussia, and Russia in January 1797 removed the name of Poland from all official usage. Although there were some attempts at resistance between 1794 and 1798, they were disorganized and easily crushed. Most of the Szlachta quickly realized that they had to adapt to the new situation if they wanted to save their fortunes and possessions. The political reality of the time pushed them into servitude to their new masters, to whom they swore loyalty. The partitioning powers were delighted to receive the submission of the Polish nobility, but they never bothered to align their policies with the ex-Polish territories. While Prussian and Austrian parts underwent strict Germanization, Catherine the Great never pursued the Russification of her part of Poland.

The only Russification attempt Catherine made was in the sphere of religion, and only towards the peasants that lived in the area of Odessa. These peasants had previously converted from Orthodoxy to Greek Catholicism, and now the empress demanded their return to Orthodoxy. Thus she created a contrast between the Catholic Lithuanian control of northern Ukraine and Orthodox southern Ukraine. This contrast would later taint all attempts to unify a national attitude towards resistance movements in Poland.

In the Prussian part of the Polish territory, the government installed a centralized administration system and the legal system already in place in Prussia. This meant that although the nobles kept most of their privileges, the serfs finally acquired some protection and were no longer exploited by their lords. The Polish education system was completely dismantled, and the German one took its place, with the German language becoming dominant. To prevent national resentment, the Prussians offered the Polish landowners the prospect of export through the Baltic ports and easily-acquired credits from Berlin banks. However, in the long run, high mortgages ruined the Polish nobility, and in time, their land passed into German hands.

The situation was similar in Austrian-controlled Poland. The administrative system was changed to a centralized, Josephinist one. Polish noble estates were reclassified to adjust to the Austrian model, with appropriate titles. Polish schools were transformed into Austrian, with heavy censorship. The Krakow university was changed into a German-Latin institute. Austria wanted to create a base of Galician peasants loyal to the Habsburg dynasty, so they eased their labor burdens and gave the serfs limited property rights. The Roman Catholic Church continued to exist in all three parts of partitioned Poland, but it was under the strict supervision of its respective foreign rulers. The Jews of Poland were now heavily taxed, and their businesses had to comply with strict bureaucratic controls. In Austrian Poland, the Jews were even required to adopt German surnames. In Russia, they had no right of movement and had to settle only in the areas they were born in.

Yearning for Independence

The final partitioning of Poland was a shock that pushed many of the nobles out of the political scene. They proved to be quite content with the peaceful lives of their countryside estates. But not all Polish people felt content, and they proved that Poland yearned for independence. The "Golden Freedom" for which Szlachta fought for centuries was opposed to the imperial absolutism under which they were suddenly forced to live. The Polish people became only more aware of their national identity during foreign rule. The petty noblemen, who were considered free citizens in the old Commonwealth, lost that status. But they were fierce fighters for their rights and would become the main reservoir from which freedom fighters would be recruited. The international instability caused by the French Revolution and the Napoleonic Wars inspired many nobles to challenge the partition of their homeland.

The national spirit of Poland was mainly kept alive by exiled, politically inept nobles and those who fought in Austria during the Napoleonic Wars. The captured Austrian Poles were taken to Italy into Polish camps, where they were trained to serve Napoleon's army as the Polish Legions. Around 20,000 Poles were training in Italy between 1797 and 1800 and were deployed to fight against Austrians and Russians. Their deeds during the Napoleonic Wars would inspire generations of Poles to come and ignite the revolutionary spirit at home. Even the modern national anthem of Poland comes from this period of military training in Italy. Written by Józef Wybicki, the song "Poland Is Not Yet Lost" was supposed to keep the morale of the Polish Legion high. The soldiers serving under General Jan Henryk Dąbrowski sang the song to a Mazurka (upbeat folk tune) and named it "Dąbrowski's Mazurka." After the liberation of Poland in 1918, this song would become the national anthem. In Poland itself, the radicals launched several secret organizations that dreamed of a constitutional and independent Poland. One of these organizations was the Society of Polish Republicans, and they strove to combine the motive of independence with the abolishment of serfdom.

The hopes of the radical organizations at home and the Polish exiles who maintained the spirit of their nation were shattered in 1801 when France signed a peace treaty with Austria and Russia and when Napoleon Bonaparte proclaimed himself emperor. They could no longer hope France would help them march across Austria to their Polish territory and liberate it from the foreign forces that controlled it. Some of them continued to hope a peasant uprising in Poland would start and legionaries would come to help their Polish brothers. But even this hope was destroyed when

Napoleon decided to send the Polish Legions to reconquer Haiti. Only a few of them would ever come back to Europe.

But the Polish nobles continued nurturing Polish national identity, this time through legal cultural activities. In 1800, The Warsaw Society of Friends of Learning was organized, and it gathered Poland's leading artists, writers, and scholars. Its main goal was to make the Polish language a major (if not the main) part of the school system in ex-Polish territories. At the same time, Princess Izabela Czartoryska opened the first Polish museum, which at the time was completely dedicated to the Polish past. Her husband, Adam Kazimierz Czartoryski, was a personal friend of Russian Prince Alexander, and it is possible he influenced the prince's views of the Polish. Alexander kept criticizing his mother, Catherine the Great, for her treatment of the Polish.

When Alexander became the Russian tsar, he recognized the plights of the Polish nobility and, in 1803, appointed Adam Czartoryski the head of Wilno University (in today's Vilnius, Lithuania). Wilno became the center of Polish-Lithuanian secondary education, completely free of Russification. However, nothing was done for the Lithuanian communities, and the preservation of the Lithuanian language fell into the hands of local, non-Polish bishops and priests. The university at Wilno quickly became the largest university in the Russian Empire and a beacon of Polish intellectual life. Due to these educational freedoms, Russia became the least evil of the three partitioning powers.

Prussian Polish territories erupted in uprising once Napoleonic forces overran Berlin in 1806. The earlier hopes of French assistance with the resistance were rekindled, but the war dragged on, and Napoleon couldn't offer the Poles any substantial help. Nevertheless, he did allow them to organize the Polish administration in the Prussian part of Poland and revived the Polish army so it could serve under his command. Prince Józef Poniatowski took command of the Polish army, setting himself for the future in which he would be regarded as a national hero and a symbol of Polish military valor during the Napoleonic Wars.

The creation of the Polish government and the revival of its army was a great prospect, and it boosted the morale of the Polish troops. However, the survival of that government completely depended on the final outcome of the war. When Napoleon and Tsar Alexander I finally signed a peace treaty on June 14, 1807, Prussian Poland was given the status of a duchy, known as the Duchy of Warsaw. Danzig was a free city once again, but Russia annexed Białystok, a city in northeastern Poland, and the surrounding area. In 1809, France and Austria were at war. At its conclusion, the Duchy of Warsaw gained half of Austrian-controlled Poland, including the cities of Krakow and Lublin.

The Duchy of Warsaw functioned as a French satellite, and Napoleon used it as a base from which he drew recruits for his wars. The army of the Duchy followed Napoleon on his expeditions to conquer Spain and later Russia (1812). The constitution of the Duchy was dictated by Napoleon, and a French-style centralized government was set in place. Even though it was a French creation and used by Napoleon as he pleased, the Duchy renewed the hope of an independent Poland and shattered the system created by the Third Partitioning. The Duchy of Warsaw was comprised of only one-fifth of the previous Polish territory, but it did encompass the Polish heartland. Napoleon respected the Polish tradition by elevating Frederick Augustus I of Saxony to the position of Grand Duke and organizing the bicameral Sejm.

The Duchy also injected modern elements into the very traditional Polish society. The Napoleonic Code, a set of French laws that Warsaw had to accept, abolished serfdom and introduced legal equality for all people. Civil marriages and divorces were now allowed, non-nobles gained the right to vote and take up governmental offices, and elementary schooling was expanded. The result was the growth of modern professional intelligentsia and a narrowing social gap between the aristocracy and the urban middle class. Still, the land magnates got to keep the rights to all arable land, while the peasants, although free, were demoted to the landless class. They were now tenants, and forced labor didn't go away. The Jews lost all their political rights for ten years, as the government decided they had failed to integrate into Polish society.

When the war between France and Russia broke out in 1812, the Duchy of Warsaw was certain that the Kingdom of Poland would be fully restored. But these hopes died quickly once France suffered a terrible defeat in Russia and Alexander I became the arbiter of the Polish future. Once Napoleon abdicated on April 6, 1814, Tsar Alexander immediately claimed the Duchy of Warsaw. He wanted to revive the Kingdom of Poland but model it after the Russian Romanov dynasty. Napoleon lost a war to the same forces that partitioned Poland, and it was very unrealistic of Poles to hope they would gain independence and the borders of Poland before 1772.

The partitioning powers were also aware that the Polish national spirit was now very strong, and it would be impossible to restore and maintain stability in the region if they didn't make some concessions to the Poles. Alexander I wanted to win the Poles to his side, so he proposed a constitutional Poland under his rule. He wanted a similar model for Russia, and he thought Poland would be an excellent test subject before making such reforms in his empire. However, he faced international opposition, especially from Austria and Great Britain. These countries feared Russian extension and advocated for the partition of the Duchy of Warsaw. The tsar had to abandon Poznan, Torun, and Krakow in return for foreign powers' acceptance of the Kingdom of Poland under Romanov rule. The so-called Congress Kingdom of Poland emerged in 1815 after the Congress of Vienna, but it was smaller than the Duchy of Warsaw by 30 percent.

The territories once ruled by the Polish kings remained fragmented, a mosaic of six administrative units: Austrian Galicia, the free city of Krakow, Prussian west Prussia, the Duchy of Posen under Prussian rule, the western gubernia (governorate) of the Russian Empire, and the autonomous Congress Kingdom of Poland. These frontiers in Poland, established by the foreign powers, would last for a century. Krakow was the only exception, as it would pass into Austrian rule after the Austro-Prussian war of 1866. All in all, the settlement of 1815 brought improvements to Polish national interests. Although fragmented, Slavonic sentimentality was maintained and even on the rise across ex-Polish territories.

Poland in the Era of Enlightenment

Russian Emperor Alexander I must take all the credit for preserving Poland as a state after the Napoleonic Wars. He kept the constitution brought by Napoleon and the French legal system. Nothing much changed for the Polish leaders, and they easily transitioned from French to Russian rule. Alexander's behavior led them to believe that the tsar would continue to be generous and that his western gubernia would one day become an integral part of the Kingdom of Poland, just as he promised in 1815. Many Poles saw Russia as a defender of Polish national interests. The influence of Alexander was vast, and the Prussian and Austrian rulers recognized the importance of preserving Polish national identity in their parts of fragmented Poland. They took a number of steps to preserve it, mainly through the installment of Polish education, scholarship, and cultural life.

In November of 1815, Alexander I was still considered the harbinger of liberty and patriotism when he gave Poland a new liberal constitution. The Congress Kingdom was now a unique place with an elected parliament and extensive civil rights. The fact that the Russian emperor could advance Poland to the level of a true European kingdom is astonishing, especially when his empire was drowned in absolutism and autocracy. But in time, Alexander proved his vision of liberty was very narrow. The Sejm had no control over the military budget, which drained most of the Kingdom's revenues. The tsar also created a mechanism by which he could supervise and directly control the Congress Kingdom. The post of the viceroy was always given to the most obedient individuals, and the tsar installed his ill-tempered brother, the Grand Duke Constantine, as the supreme officer of the Polish army. The Russian Empire also introduced preventive censorship in Poland, and the western gubernia was never attached to the Kingdom.

All three foreign powers that controlled Polish territories implemented certain political restrictions in 1819. Though mild, these restrictions provoked discontent among the Poles in the Congress Kingdom, especially among the gentry liberals led by the Niemojowski brothers. They campaigned to defend the constitution, but in 1820, Alexander I warned the Poles not to overstep the boundaries of the liberty that was given to them. He threatened he would authorize his brother, Constantine, to use any means necessary to maintain order. The parliament had no sessions until 1825, and even then, the discussions were closed to the public. All those who advocated the ideas of Enlightenment were under direct attack by the loyalists. At first, the tsar encouraged the founding of secret societies that would promote the ideas of liberalism, but after 1820, he called for their closing as well as the closing of patriotic societies that committed their work to Polish education and promoting national reunification.

In 1825, Alexander I was succeeded by his younger brother, Nicholas I. With his accession, Polish-Russian relations quickly deteriorated. Tsar Nicholas made it clear that the western gubernia would never join the Congress Kingdom, smashing all the hopes Poland had for expansion to the east. He also accused and tried the National Patriotic Society of being connected with Russian

Decembrists, a revolt that occurred after the sudden death of Alexander I. When the Polish High Tribunal failed to sentence its members because it was not willing to dash the hope of possible reunification, Nicholas wanted to override their decision. This would be unconstitutional, and a crisis would emerge. But the tsar never had the chance to fulfill his threats, as the new war with Turkey (1828-1829) erupted and his attention was drawn to the front.

Despite the absolutist tendencies of Tsar Nicholas I, a period of political stability started in Poland. Due to the Congress Kingdom's energetic finance minister, Franciszek Ksawery Drucki-Lubecki, the Kingdom bloomed economically. The minister reformed the taxation system, promoted the opening of the Polish National Bank, and reformed the cotton, mining, and ironworks industries. Although he started the modernization of the Kingdom, his deeds undermined the efforts of national solidarity. The fiscal reforms of Drucki-Lubecki were harsh on peasants who were already suffering. Their numbers rose, and they were still forced to be tenants while the land available to them was growing smaller. Likewise, the Polish peasants grew while they continued to be deprived of the constitutional civil rights the Poles enjoyed.

The Congress Kingdom wasn't the only part of historic Poland that was endowed with autonomy. The free city of Krakow obtained a liberal, though aristocratic, constitution and retained the Napoleonic legal system. The three partitioning powers continued to interfere in the policies of Krakow, undermining its liberalization, but the city continued to be free until 1846. The peasants of the Krakow region had the best status of all the historic Polish regions, with the security of tenancy holding and electoral rights. This means that in Krakow, the rural population became politically aware and involved. Industrially, Krakow wasn't as developed as the Congress Kingdom, but the first steam engine in Poland was installed there in 1817.

The ex-Polish territories under Prussian control had a more complex history. In Poznan, the degree of autonomy was low, but the Prussian authorities didn't want to antagonize the Poles and were aware that the Congress Kingdom was a much more attractive solution. To keep the peace, they made Polish the main language of the Poznan courts, administration, and schools. They placed Prince Anthony Radziwiłł as viceroy of Poznania. As for the peasants in Prussian-controlled parts of Poland, the process of creating peasant farmers was in motion, although the nobility remained the majority owners of the land.

In West Prussia (once Polish Pomerania), no significant concessions were made toward Polish nationality. Although the Polish people represented half of West Prussia, the majority of towns were German, and the landed class was becoming majorly German, too. In 1824, East and West Prussia became one entity, and the restoration of Malbork Castle became a symbol of Teutonic German Prussia. Nevertheless, Prussia failed to stop the emergence of Polish national consciousness in the regions they controlled. Even the Polish communities of Upper Silesia and Masurian East Prussia, which were never part of the Polish-Lithuanian Commonwealth, would fall under the influence of Polish patriotism.

The November Uprising of 1830

Despite various restrictions imposed on ex-Polish territories by the partitioning powers, Poland became a European learning center. In the realms of philosophy, art, and literature, Polish intellectuals were heavily influenced by their peers across borders. Despite the interference of the censors, foreign thought managed to penetrate and enter Polish society, especially western Romanticism and German idealism. The younger generations of the Congress Kingdom were impressed and inspired by the new philosophies. They started questioning the old values of the Polish elite and celebrating the heroic actions of defiance. Young Poles across the Kingdom and the western gubernia cherished the concept of

Romanticism, in which a nation is a moral community always striving for self-fulfillment. The University of Warsaw started harnessing the ideas of democracy, and its students harbored a vision of a reunited Poland.

The Romantic dream of Polish independence found its way into the ranks of the junior military officers. They were inspired by the political upheavals of 1830 that swept Europe into a revolutionary wave. On November 29, 1830, the junior officers launched an armed insurrection against Russian authorities. They attempted to assassinate Grand Duke Constantine, but their action met utter failure. Nevertheless, they managed to seize the arsenal of Warsaw and distribute some 30,000 rifles to the city's population, securing the continuation of the revolt. The Poles that held high offices condemned the revolt and even urged the Grand Duke to use violence against the rebels. Constantine refused to listen to them and relied on Polish authorities to bring the Kingdom to order.

A new Patriotic Society was established by Maurycy Mochnacki, a powerful Romantic poet and orator who attracted the revolutionaries outside of Warsaw. The Kingdom's government failed to restore order and felt obliged to summon the Sejm. But it was too late. The Sejm was moved by the wave of patriotism and, instead of condemning, endorsed the insurrection. It appointed General Józef Chłopicki, a veteran of the Napoleonic Wars, as commander of the people. Chłopicki saw that the revolt would be futile and resigned on January 23. However, he took part in some of the battles as a common soldier. After two months of fighting Russian authorities, the Sejm was deposed by Tsar Nicholas I by public proclamation. The Sejm claimed that the tsar had violated the constitution, but it had also illegally defied the Treaty of Vienna by which Poland and Russia were united.

From the very beginning, the uprising suffered internal struggle over its nature, goals, and the methods used to achieve them. Moderate conservatives wanted to prevent radicals of the Patriotic

Society from taking all the power, and they placed one of their own as the leader of the insurrection. Adam Jerzy Czartoryski became chief of the Polish National Government in January 1831. In February, the Sejm proclaimed Poland a hereditary constitutional kingdom in which only the Sejm in session had the right to elect a new king.

Czartoryski and his associates were aware they could not secure the complete independence of Poland, but they used the uprising to secure the revision of the clauses of the Treaty of Vienna regarding Poland. They were even willing to commit to a dynastical relationship with Russia. Contrasting with the government, the radicals wanted to present the uprising of 1830 as a war of the people against the Russian oppressor. Both parties agreed that the independence of the Kingdom of Poland should be the end goal of the uprising, but the events around it extended the war effort. The revolution spread to the western gubernia, and the Polish Sejm issued a bill in May 1831 by which this vast area was added to the kingdom.

In the meantime, Tsar Nicholas I was resolved to reduce the autonomy of the Congress Kingdom of Poland. He also refused to let go of the western gubernia, and the revolution transformed from the Warsaw uprising to the full-scale Polish-Russian War of 1830-31 (November Uprising, Cadet Revolution). The Polish army numbered 80,000 well-trained and experienced men, and at the beginning of the conflict, it was very effective. Before the escalation of the war, the Polish army stopped the Russian advance on Warsaw and won the Battle of Olszynka Grochowska. In spring, the Poles made a series of successful military advances that alarmed Tsar Nicholas. Russia sent the experienced general Ivan Paskevich to lead the army across the Vistula near the Prussian border and approach Warsaw from the west. The Polish government saw the upcoming defeat, and Czartoryski suggested seeking protection from Austria. But his governmental associates didn't want outside help. Their inability to decide how to respond to the Russian threat led to the government's resignation in August. Although the uprising was a lost cause, the Polish military leaders refused to capitulate to Russia. They preferred self-exile.

The main reason for Poland's failure is that it had no political unity, and the leadership they organized doubted the success of the uprising. Wide social support was also lacking, and there were no imaginative ideas on how to win the war against a mightier enemy. The peasant masses were not inspired to fight, given their dependent status in the Polish Kingdom. Even when the Sejm promised them the possibility of purchasing land, they were not inspired. Polish leadership also refused to invest in gaining international support, which could bring them victory. Unlike Polish leadership, the people of Britain, Germany, and France urged their governments to act. They fully supported the national interest of Poland and hoped for their independence. But the foreign governments were not moved, and the cabinets of Vienna and Berlin remained stubbornly neutral, while the French and British ones were preoccupied with domestic matters.

Poland paid a grave cost of defeat. The dream of a large, reunited, and independent Poland was shattered. It also lost all the gains of 1815. Nicholas I abolished the constitution, the Sejm, and the Polish army. He also closed the University of Warsaw, and the Kingdom was placed under Russian occupation. In 1833, a citadel prison for political enemies was built in the capital, and martial law was introduced. The statehood of the Congress Kingdom of Poland was over. Prussia and Austria felt encouraged to remove some of the concessions they made towards the Poles, all under the pretense of fear of Polish nationalism.

In 1883/4, all three partitioning powers signed a mutual agreement by which they promised to respect and guarantee their Polish territories. They committed themselves to the suppression of all revolutionary sentiments that might have lingered after the

November Uprising. Even the papal office condemned the revolution, wishing to preserve the social and political order in Europe. The closing of the Polish schools and universities was the biggest blow to Polish culture, yet it was only the beginning of the upcoming Russification.

But not all hope was lost. Some 10,000 Polish exiles left their country and headed west. They promoted Russophobia and the image of a heroic Poland as a victim of the totalitarian and tyrannical regime of Russia. Western liberals and radicals were quick to adopt Russophobia. The exiles were free in the west, and they could spend their time plotting and envisioning a liberated Poland. They spent the next decade and a half spreading the Romantic idea of freedom for their country, and they helped preserve the Polish national consciousness.

Chapter 7 – The Revolution and Transformation (1848-1918)

A textile factory in Łódź, a symbol of modernization in Poland
*https://en.wikipedia.org/wiki/Congress_Poland#/media/File:Bronis%C5%82aw_Wilkoszew
ski_%E2%80%93_Fabryka_Tow._Ak._Pozna%C5%84skicgo.jpg*

In a way, Polish exiled intellectuals, artists, poets, and writers predicted the revolutionary wave that would crash on Europe in 1848. More than ten thousand political opponents, military elite, and artists were exiled from Poland after the November Revolution. In their host countries, they started promoting the Polish national consciousness and spreading Russophobia. They thought of themselves as the soul of the Polish nation, the exiled revolutionaries who had suffered under unjust Russian rule. They started expressing their revolutionary ideas through their work in foreign lands. In his work "Books of the Polish Nation and Polish Pilgrimage," poet and principal figure of Polish Romanticism Adam Bernard Mickiewicz wrote that everyone should prepare for the upcoming war for the freedom of people. Between 1840 and 1844, he worked at the Collège de France, where his lectures started attacking the existing world order and calling for its downfall.

Famous composer Frédéric Chopin composed his Étude Op. 10, No. 12 between 1830 and 1832. Although it is unknown if the piece was inspired by the events of the November Revolution, many of his contemporaries felt the revolutionary spirit in this piece of music. This piece is also called the "Revolutionary Étude" and "Étude on the Bombardment of Warsaw." Chopin neither confirmed nor denied if he drew the inspiration from the events in Poland, but his music is certainly the purest expression of the Polish Romantic feeling. Similar feelings were expressed in his later compositions of mazurkas and krakowiaks. Although Chopin never participated in the revolution since he left Poland for France in 1829, his work inspired the national and revolutionary consciousness of Poles across the world. Rightfully so, this composer became a sacred national icon.

Adam Jerzy Czartoryski continued supporting constitutional monarchy from Paris, his place of exile. He founded a political group of moderate conservative and liberal Poles in exile in France. He was already a renowned politician and kept his contacts with the French and British governments and a network of agents across Europe. He used his power and influence to defend Polish national rights as defined by the participation treaties of 1815, but soon he expanded his political program into openly supporting another revolt. However, he was aware that for the next revolt to support, it needed to meet two conditions: it had to coincide with a major war between Russia and another European power, and it had to have the support of the peasants, who constituted the majority of the population.

Czartoryski compelled his international agents to weaken the Russian influence on the Balkans and promote national awakening. He also persuaded the papal office in Rome to change its stance on Polish nationalism and embrace it as a positive and progressive influence. However, most of the exiled Poles didn't want to be part of Czartoryski's scheme, no matter how much he advocated for the cause. They found him too aristocratic, especially his view that the Szlachta was an integral part of the Polish culture and that the nobles were essential to the national cause.

Another Polish political group known as the Polish Democratic Society was founded in Paris in 1832. It called for the removal of all social privileges and the equality of all citizens. Soon, the Polish Democratic Society realized they could achieve nothing without the support of the Szlachta, but it never gave up insisting that the peasants must gain the right to own property without paying an indemnity. A third group that established itself in Portsmouth, the Commune of the Polish People, consisted of exiled officers and soldiers. They openly called for the overthrow of the nobility, collective land ownership, and the rejection of industrialization. But such agrarian socialism never took hold in Poland, and the Commune found itself isolated and weakened by internal struggles.

All active exiled groups accepted the need for the involvement of peasants in the next uprising and fight for independence. But they had to act fast to inspire the peasants, as they feared the partitioning powers would improve the peasants' social standing and well-being. Peasants would be content with their lives and have no reason to join an insurrection. This was the reality they had to fight, especially because these exiled political groups were seen as a peripheral element in the daily lives and concerns of all Poles who remained in partitioned Poland, not just the peasants.

The Struggle for Independence

All the political groups and movements that advocated for the national and social liberation of Poland failed to do anything of significance until the 1840s. There was no major European war or the great rising of the people of Europe, but they patiently waited and continued challenging the political and social order in Poland. Prince Czartoryski continued spreading his influence and propaganda, and the Polish Democratic Society established a vast underground network in Poland. In Russian and Austrian Poland, a new generation of young radicals was ready for a change, and they set to work from within. One of these radicals, Edward Dembowski—a nobleman, philosopher, and journalist—often dressed as a peasant and went from village to village to spread the idea of revolution.

The Polish Democratic Society heard of Dembowski's efforts and realized that the peasants were almost ready to voice their discontent through an insurrection. They quickly took it upon themselves to channel this discontent of the peasants into a national cause. They had no time to waste and planned for the revolution to start in 1846, with exiled general Ludwik Mierosławski taking command of the people's army. Czartoryski urged the nobility to join the revolution. He didn't intend for it to happen so soon, but he was unable to stop it. None of the groups involved managed to recognize how deeply divided the Polish peasantry was, and soon this would cost them their revolution.

The cultural, social, and political fissures between peasants in Austrian, Prussian, and Russian-controlled parts of Poland were too deep. Mierosławski and his Democrats were betrayed by the Prussian peasants before they could take their first revolutionary action. The Russians became aware of the revolutionary sentiment in the Kingdom and quickly acted to suppress it. Only in free

Krakow did the peasants rally in support of the revolution. In the western part of Galicia, the Catholic peasants not only betrayed the rebels but joined the Austrians in the killing spree. While trying to win over the Galician peasants, Dembowski was killed just outside of Krakow. Once it finished dealing with the revolution of 1846, Austria annexed the free city of Krakow with Russian and Prussian consent.

But when the revolutionary wave of 1848/9 washed over Europe, the Polish exiles found new hope and a new motivation to fight for Poland's independence. During the "Springtime of the Peoples," the Russian part of Poland was at peace, as Tsar Nicholas tightened his repressive control and killed off any thought of insurrection among the Polish citizens. In Prussia and Austria, absolutism collapsed, and the rebels had much greater chances of succeeding there. Mierosławski, who had spent time in Berlin's prison since 1846, was now free and set to organizing the Polish army and administration in Poznania.

The new liberal government of Prussia was even willing to step into an alliance with the Poles, and they also had the support of revolutionary France. However, this alliance never concluded, as Prussia was unwilling to attack Russia and fight for Polish freedom beyond the borders of Poznania. Although the Poles enjoyed the support of the German and French people, the governments of these two countries were unwilling to start another major war in Europe for Poland's independence.

In Galicia, the memories of the massacre and annexation of Krakow were still fresh. So, when the Revolutions of 1848 spread to Vienna, the Poles did nothing more than petition for the autonomy of their province. Only Krakow dared to rise against Austrian rule, but on April 26, the city was bombarded into submission. The Austrian emperor once again won over the Galician peasants by abolishing the corvée (unpaid forced labor), thus preventing their participation in the revolution. But the revolutionary sentiment was strong in Vienna, and the Poles of Galicia and Krakow felt encouraged to continue their efforts. They created a national guard with 20,000 men serving it. Their leaders hoped Galicia would become a center of Polish freedom and independence from where they could launch operations to free other parts of historic Poland.

But the Galician Poles found trouble in their eastern region, where the Ukrainian national movement had just established itself. The Ukrainians of Galicia demanded Austrian imperial protection against the rebellious Poles and eventual division of the province along ethnic lines. But the Austrian government only exploited the ethnic conflict between the Poles and Ukrainians. By November 1848, Austria restored full control over Galicia and suppressed any attempt at revolution. The Polish fighters who survived the conflict with Austria fled across the Carpathians to help the Hungarians in their fight with the Habsburgs. This fight was more fruitful than the Polish one, and the Austrians soon had to turn to Russia for help. Russia obliged its ally, mostly because the tsar feared any nationalist awakening in Europe, believing it would spread to the Russian-controlled part of Poland. The Russian army crushed the Hungarian rebellion within three months.

The Poles didn't fight only in Poland. Their contributions to the revolutions in France, Italy, Hungary, and Germany are significant. Their slogan for the international fight was "For Your Freedom and Ours." But it soon became clear that the Polish Romantic thought of European brotherhood and friendship between the nations was just a dream. There was no outside help coming to fight for Polish independence. However, the events of 1848/9 served to strengthen the Polish spirit. In both Prussian and Austrian areas, Polish journalism and debate around Polish independence flourished. The Poznanian peasants displayed a will to join the national cause, and that was a clear sign that Polish nationalism among them was growing. Even the peasants of Silesia started re-awakening attachment to their Polish language. Only the peasants of Galicia remained loyal to Austrian imperialism, but even there, the process of their integration into the wider Polish community had begun.

Polish nationalism was on the rise, but the cultural, social, and political divide between the different parts of Poland was too wide and could not be ignored. The partition powers continued to be strong allies and slowly silenced the revolutionary exiles. Within Poland, the educated people started resenting the exiles' claim that they were guiding the national spirit. Instead, they turned to non-revolutionary methods of self-preservation. In Prussian areas, the Polish aristocracy started attending the parliament established in 1851, while in Austrian Galicia, a Polish viceroy was chosen. There the aristocracy advocated loyalism to the Habsburg dynasty.

In the Russian areas, conditions for the Poles and the Jews were relaxed with the reforms introduced by the new Tsar Alexander II. He suspended military recruiting, gave amnesty to political prisoners, opened a medical academy in Warsaw, and allowed Count Andrzej Zamoyski to establish the Agricultural Society that gathered the old landed nobility of Poland. The Agricultural Society quickly transformed into a national forum for the moderate opinion, and its representatives assumed some of the powers of the old Polish Sejm. Encouraged by the existence of this society, the Poles started asking for a local government and wider social reforms. But for Tsar Alexander II, this was pushing it too far. Although he was willing to introduce some reforms and even lift the censorship of the Polish press, he was afraid of encouraging the uprising.

During 1859 and 1860, Warsaw saw many demonstrations as people took to the streets and demanded more freedoms from the Russian government. They started singing patriotic songs in the streets and churches, calling for rebellion. In 1861, the events became violent, and Russian authorities even opened fire on the demonstrators, killing five people. The tsar was now resolved to crush all social unrest and calls for independence in his part of

Poland. The Agricultural Society was shut down, and the churches were closed because they promoted unrest. The people took their displeasure with Russian authorities to the streets and started praying and revolting against such measures. They were on their knees when the Russian regiment opened fire on them and killed around 100 people before dispersing the crowd.

But while Zamoyski and his followers advocated the peaceful expansion of Polish rights within the Russian Empire, a new generation of radicals was establishing itself. They were styled "the Reds," and they expanded their network outside of Poland. Inspired by the events in Russian Poland, the Reds started preparing for an uprising. They established connections with the radicals within the Russian tsarist army and with the Italian troops that served under General Ludwik Mierosławski.

But in 1862, Tsar Alexander II decided to grant the Congress Kingdom of Poland a certain level of self-rule. The new archbishop of Warsaw was elected, signaling an improving relationship between the Catholic Church and the Russian government. Liberal-minded Constantine, the younger brother of the tsar, was appointed viceroy of Poland, and a new civilian government was elected to deal with all non-military matters. The new government immediately started social and educational reforms. The Jews finally obtained equal rights as the Poles, but the relationship between nobility and peasantry remained a problem. The pleas of the peasantry for the ownership of land were not fulfilled.

But the Reds demanded the extension of political liberties for the Poles. When nothing was done to secure them, they intensified their preparation for a revolt. Their leader, Jarosław Dąbrowski, established a Central National Committee that controlled all the underground actions of the revolutionaries. A new paramilitary force was gathered with the assignment of assassinating the new viceroy, Constantine. Zamoyski worked to appease the Reds, and in September of 1862, he proposed to Constantine to merge the western gubernia with the Kingdom. He was exiled for daring to propose such a thing. But the tsar and his brother failed to see that Zamoyski leaving Poland meant the dissolution of the party that wanted peaceful collaboration with Russian authorities.

The Polish government, under the leadership of Alexander Wielopolski, ordered the conscription of some 12,000 Polish radicals into the tsarist army. By this, they hoped to dilute the ranks of the Reds and prevent their rebellion. However, they only managed to force their hand. On January 22, 1863, the Central National Committee proclaimed itself the Interim National Government of the Kingdom of Poland and declared war against Russia. At first, the rebels had only around 6,000 armed men capable of fighting. They faced the Russian army of 100,000 men stationed in the Kingdom, with more available from the western gubernia. The Interim Government hoped they could quickly win over the urban and peasant masses by granting them full property rights. Mierosławski was proclaimed a dictator, but even he failed to gather more than 30,000 able-bodied men. The Polish insurrection turned into a guerilla war.

The hit-and-run tactics of Mierosławski's army proved efficient against the massive Russian army. Their fight in the forests of Poland and Lithuania inspired great international support and even official protests in St. Petersburg by the British and French governments. But the insurgents were delusional to think international help was on its way. Their fight only persuaded those who had previously opposed the war against Russia. Many volunteers from Galicia and Poznania crossed the border to help their compatriots, and the insurrection spread to western Belorussia and engulfed Lithuania. But in Ukraine, the people were not willing to join the fight.

Yet Polish insurgents were unable to fight the mighty Russian army alone. They prolonged the guerilla war until March 1864, when the last hope of international military help, or at least a

European Congress that would deal with the Polish question, died. The Russian government not only fought the insurgents but also launched heavy propaganda to win over the hearts and minds of the Polish peasants. Tsar Alexander initiated a land reform promising the same freedoms to the peasants as the Interim Government. Support for the revolution quickly died out in the countryside, which enabled the authorities to find and arrest the leaders of the insurrection. The remaining revolutionaries were quickly dealt with, although the last fighting regiment held out until 1865.

Many insurgents were executed, but an even greater number were sent to Siberia, where they would pay their penalty for the rest of their lives. Yet another attempt to challenge the partition of Poland had failed. But the January Uprising and the Interim National Government that smoothly operated right under the nose of the tsarist authorities became a symbol of national aspiration across 19th century Europe. For over eighteen months, the guerilla insurgents resisted the largest European army. Destined to fail from the beginning, the Poles displayed incredible strength of heart and mind against an overwhelming enemy. The era of Romanticism ended and, with it, the dream of Polish independence. The question that remained was for how long.

The Transformation

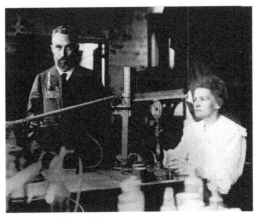

Marie Curie and her husband Pierre Curie in their laboratory, circa 1904
https://en.wikipedia.org/wiki/Marie_Curie#/media/File:Pierre_and_Marie_Curie.jpg

After the insurrection of 1863/4 was crushed, Russia decided to fully incorporate the Congress Kingdom into its empire. Poland was renamed Vistula Land (*Privislinsky Krai*), and the office of viceroy was abolished. The names "Russian Poland" and "the Congress Kingdom" were still in official use, but the once-independent kingdom had now completely lost its autonomy. With the outbreak of the Russo-Turkish war in 1877, the Polish question as an international issue was pushed aside. Russia and Prussia dedicated themselves to further weakening Polish national character and limiting the social freedoms of Poles. Russian became the official language of administration, and censorship was reintroduced. In the western gubernia, the Polish language was completely banned, and the Polish people were prohibited from buying land there.

The Polish educational system was not spared either. By 1885, the Polish language was replaced by obligatory Russian in elementary and secondary schools. Women were not allowed to enroll in universities, and Warsaw's university was closed and replaced by a Russian one. Poles wanted to learn their own language, Polish history, and Catholicism, but these subjects were illegal. In 1885, an underground educational institution, the Flying University (*Uniwersytet Latający*), started operating in Warsaw. Here, the Poles were given an education similar to the traditional teaching of the old Polish educational system. Although the education received at the Flying University wasn't official, it allowed the Polish youth to resist Russification. A similar underground university operated in the Prussian part of Poland to resist the Germanization of Poles.

One prominent student of Flying University at Warsaw was Maria Salomea Skłodowska, later known by her French name Marie Curie. Because she was a woman, the Russian authorities didn't allow her to attend higher education. Eager to learn, Maria attended underground lessons while working as a governess to finance her sister's medical education in Paris. A few years later, her sister hosted her in France, enabling Maria to enroll in a French university and finish her studies in physics, mathematics, and chemistry. Although she settled in France and married a fellow scientist, Pierre Curie, Maria always dreamed of going back to Poland. She even married Pierre only once he declared he would follow her to her home country. Their research on radiation brought them Nobel Prize in 1903. In 1911, she won her second Nobel Prize in Chemistry (she discovered the element radium). She was not only the first woman to receive the Nobel Prize but also the first person to receive it twice in two different fields. Sadly, her dream to return to Poland would never come true. But she visited her home country often and even established Warsaw Radium Institute in 1932. Her last visit to Poland was in 1934, only several months before her death.

In Prussian-controlled Poland, the suppression of Polish culture resembled what was happening in Russian-controlled areas. Poznania and West Prussia (Danzig Pomerania) had been excluded from the German Confederation founded in 1815. Now, they were fully integrated into Germany, and the German language became the official administrative language. By 1887, it also became an official language in all schools. German statesman Otto von Bismarck wanted to eradicate Polish nationalism, and he thought the only way to do that was to subordinate the Roman Catholic Church to the German state. Many monasteries and churches of Poznań-Gniezno were dissolved, and priests were arrested. Even Archbishop Mieczysław Halka-Ledóchowski spent two years in prison before being exiled to Rome. But what Bismarck failed to predict was that his crack on the Catholic Church would only strengthen the ties between religion and nationalism, between Catholicism and Polish national identity.

In the nineteenth century, Austria treated its Polish citizens very differently than Prussia and Russia. The Habsburg Empire was greatly weakened as it suffered defeats from France in 1859 and

Prussia in 1866. Vienna was obliged to make constitutional concessions and develop the Council of State and regional parliaments. Polish Galicia was given a degree of autonomy within the Austro-Hungarian Empire, with which its conservative Polish leaders were satisfied. The local elite acquired control of internal affairs in Galicia, and the post of viceroy and minister of Galicia was always given to Poles, at least up until 1918. The Poles were also chosen as Galician representatives to the central Austrian parliament, and several Polish individuals held Austrian high offices. Count Alfred Potocki was the first Pole to hold the office of prime minister (1870-71). In Austria, traditional Polish culture flourished, and the Polish language became one of the official languages of Austrian administration, schools, and universities.

The last decades of the 18th century saw the industrialization of Polish territories controlled by the three partitioning powers. But the level of industrialization was nowhere near that of Prussia, Russia, and Austria. Railway was introduced to enable the economic growth of the controlling powers, not Poland itself. Poland remained largely a country of peasants and agricultural producers. Nevertheless, with industrialization came new ideologies and political movements. Polish society accepted socialism, modern nationalism, and agrarian populism—popular ideologies in central and eastern Europe in the late 19th century. A new generation of radical youth was established, and they clashed with the Polish nobility that wanted to peacefully coexist with the partitioning powers.

Modern Polish socialism started developing in the 1870s, and it drew its ideas from Karl Marx, Friedrich Engels, and the native insurrectionary history of Romantic Poland. The first Marxist group was founded in 1882 by Ludwik Waryński, but it was quickly broken by the Russian authorities. Socialist ideas continue to live among the Polish abroad. In 1892, the Polish Socialist Party (PPS) was established in Paris with Józef Piłsudski (1867-1935) as its leader. He would become a dominant figure in Polish political life after World War I. Piłsudski worked on attracting the industrial working class of Russian Poland to his revolutionary cause. He believed that socialism could be achieved only if Poland was to become independent and reunited.

But independent Poland opposed the Marxist doctrine on the nature of socialism. Rosa Luxemburg, who founded the Social Democracy of the Kingdom of Poland (SDKPiL), believed that Poland was strongly tied to Russia economically, which made the kingdom's independence impossible. By 1906, it was clear that PPS had the advantage of numbers, as they gathered 50,000 followers while SDKPiL had only around 30,000. The division among the socialists of Poland was far too great, and the two parties could never agree on the national question of Poland.

Socialism never managed to take hold among the Poles in ex-Prussia (now Germany after the unification of 1871), not in its Polish or German forms. There, Polish nationalism was bound to Catholicism, and the industrial workforce was too small to make a difference. Silesia had more industrial workers, but even there, the population tended to vote for the German Centre Party (Catholic Centre Party). In Austrian Galicia, socialism fared a little bit better. The social party managed to function legally in Austro-Hungarian Empire, though only with its non-revolutionary program. The Habsburg lands were undergoing severe fragmentation into ethnic-linguistic components, and the socialist party and its ideas of political and social rights were pushed aside.

Aside from socialism, a nationalist movement grew in Poland. Its origins can be traced to Geneva, where the Polish Union (*Liga Polska*) was founded by Zygmunt Miłkowski, and to Krakow, where Zygmunt Balicki founded the Union of Polish Youth, or the "Zet." Both of these movements were founded in 1887. However, Miłkowski's Union, although nationalist, was too liberal for all the young nationalists in Warsaw. The new generation in Poland took over the Union in 1897 and renamed it the National Democratic Party (ND), nicknamed Endecja (Polish reading of shortening ND). The National Democrats never gave up on Polish independence, but first, they wanted to preserve the Polish identity under the foreign powers, especially in the age of Russian imperialism and *Realpolitik*. They could achieve this only through further developing nationalist ideology.

Soon, the National Democrats won over the support of the Kingdom's middle class and artisans. Then they turned their focus on the countryside, where their propaganda, campaigns, and activism brought them the support of the majority of peasants. The youngsters were attracted not only to the ideas of nationalism but also to the party's youth organizations and the actions it organized. They openly opposed socialism, which only served to bring them the support of the Catholic clergy. The ND's anti-German stance ensured the support of the industrial workers of Upper Silesia and Poznania. However, they were very unpopular among non-Polish nations, especially Ukrainians and the Jews. The nationalists thought that all non-Polish had to willingly submit to the Polonization.

When the Russian Revolution started in 1905, all the Polish political parties hoped it would mean change for their kingdom. Conservative wealthy families that formed the Real Politics Party remained loyal to the Russian tsar and would be rewarded with linguistic, religious, and legal freedoms and concessions. The National Democrats hoped for the kingdom's autonomy, while the PPS believed the revolution would spread to Poland and started preparing for an uprising. But the Russian Revolution and the Russo-Japanese War (1904-1905) brought only the fall of industrial production, unemployment, and the disruption of trade in Poland. The poor harvest that year threatened famine, and the streets saw an increased number of demonstrations. Students demanded education in the Polish language, while workers entered a month-long general strike. The peasants that had just become aware of their political power also demanded the use of the Polish language in administration.

In April 1905, tsarist Russia agreed to some religious concessions and allowed somewhat wider use of the local languages. But no concessions were given to the workers, and they continued their protests. The result was an armed workers' uprising in June that resulted in hundreds of lost lives. But soon, the Russian workers entered a general strike as well, throwing the empire even deeper into revolutionary chaos. By that time, the revolution in Poland had turned into a civil war. However, Tsar Nicholas II was not prepared to give any political concessions to the Poles. In November, martial law was introduced throughout the kingdom, and the Russian army crushed all resistance.

When Tsar Nicholas II promised a constitutional order, the PPS party split into two wings. One was led by the young socialists who wanted to widen the political settlement with Russia but remain part of the empire. The second part was made of old socialists who demanded nothing less than an independent Poland under socialist order. In November 1906, the split of the PPS became official, creating the young "Left" and the old socialists regrouped in the "Revolutionary Faction." But none of the Polish political parties managed to secure the fulfillment of their objectives during the revolutionary period of 1905. Poland continued to be part of the Russian Empire, although the Polish language entered wider use, and the Poles were once again allowed to buy property in the western gubernia. The National Democrats even managed to enter Duma, the Russian Parliament. Small concessions that Russia agreed to kept the Polish spirit alive.

In Galicia, the revolutionary spirit was kept alive among the Poles who managed to bring democratization to the Austrian electoral system. In 1907, universal male suffrage was introduced for the central parliament in Vienna. Austrian Galicia had much better conditions for the Poles, and it was the place where Russian exiles sought refuge. In Galicia, they were able to express their political views without being persecuted by the tsarist authorities. They could study in the Polish language, and education was available to both sexes. This is where the leader of the PPS, Józef Piłsudski, found a new audience for his socialist ideology.

In Prussian Poland, the German-Polish struggle continued with the same vigor as ever. The Poles were forbidden from building on newly-purchased land, and their language never entered administration or education. Some of the towns in Pomerania and Poznania even received new German names. Berlin allowed only Germans to permanently settle in the eastern provinces, but ironically, the Germans found western parts of their country more attractive, as they had better economic prospects. A desperate government even passed a bill in 1908 that allowed the Germans to forcefully buy Polish-owned land.

As 1914 approached, bringing major European conflict that would grow into World War I, Poland was as divided as ever. Not only was it partitioned between Germany, Russia, and Austria, but it was also culturally, socially, and politically divided. Not a single region could claim it was exclusively homogenous in terms of religion, ethnicity, or language. There was no more Poland, and it is a miracle the nation survived the period of partition, let alone maintained the dream of independence. In fact, despite the division that destroyed Poland as a state, the Polish national consciousness managed to spread. When World War I started, 15.5 million Polish-speaking people were settled around the Vistula and Warta rivers, 1.3 million in eastern Galicia, and 2 million in Russia's western gubernia.

But the language wasn't the only link that kept all the divided Poles together. Their culture, although diverse in different parts of historical Poland, shared a love for Romantic literature. Polish readers celebrated the lives and works of great writers. The famous

Adam Mickiewicz had his statue erected in Warsaw, Lwow, and Krakow. Henryk Sienkiewicz won the Noble Prize in Literature in 1905, celebrated equally in the Austrian, Prussian, and Russian parts of Poland. Another cultural link was the Catholic Church, which played an enormous role in keeping Polish society unified. Catholicism kept the Poles separate from the Protestant Prussians and Orthodox Russians. The unity of Polish Catholic society was especially felt in annual pilgrimages to the Shrine of the Black Madonna in Częstochowa and the Shrine of Our Lady of Ostra Brama in Wilno. These pilgrimages were made by the people from all three parts of Poland and presented them with the opportunity to meet and keep their distinct Polish character.

Chapter 8 – Poland in World Wars

Polish defense line during the invasion of 1939
Fair use under US copyright law;
https://en.wikipedia.org/wiki/History_of_Poland_(1939%E2%80%931945)#/media/File:Polish_infantr
y.jpg

Independence Gained

With the outbreak of World War I, the partitioning powers found themselves against each other for the first time since the destruction of the Polish-Lithuanian Republic. Germany and Austria-Hungary (Central Powers) fought against Russia and its allies, France and Great Britain (Triple Entente). Previous Polish revolutionaries believed that Poland's independence could come only from a major European war. But none of the old insurgents were alive now to take the reins and unite Poland. In fact, at the outbreak of the Great War, Poland was bitterly divided. Józef Piłsudski and his followers were pro-German and believed that the future of Poland lay within Germany. He also hoped that Austria-Hungary would agree to make their dual kingdom into a triple one: Austria-Hungary-Poland. To achieve this, he believed he needed to help his fellow Germans defeat Russia.

But Piłsudski's opponents in the National Democratic Party were against his anti-Russian campaigns. They were attracted to the manifesto issued by Russian commander-in-chief, Grand Duke Nicholas Nikolaevich, which called for a unified Poland that would have full autonomy within the Russian Empire. Nicholas Nicholaevich even formed a Polish legion within the Russian army to counter Piłsudski's legion that fought on the German side. The Polish people found themselves killing each other instead of working on unification. The economic resources of the territory of historic Poland were exploited by both warring sides. The eastern front ran right through the Polish territory.

In 1915, the Central Powers managed to take over the whole front and occupy what was once the Polish Kingdom. All the territories that were once under tsarist Russia, including the capital Warsaw, found themselves under the control of the Central Powers. Over one million Poles retreated to Russia with the tsarist army, fearing repression under the German boot. The majority of the Polish National Democrats, together with their leader Roman

Dmowski, left for St. Petersburg, now renamed Petrograd so the city would lose the German parts of the name. But many Russian supporters were left behind and were eventually sent to German labor camps in the west. Those who Russian authorities considered traitors and German collaborators were arrested and transported to the east, probably even to Siberia.

Dmowski tirelessly lobbied in St. Petersburg for the tsarist government to resolve the issue of Poland. But the Russian Empire was preoccupied with the war it seemed to be losing, and Polish pleas landed on deaf ears. Dmowski left Russia to persuade Britain and France to urge their ally to make some concessions to Poland. In the meantime, the German government started wooing the Poles with the promise of making Polish the official language in education, administration, and the courts. They even reopened some of the old Polish universities. Piłsudski's idea of Habsburg Poland even reached Vienna, where it was seriously considered. But Germany intervened and persuaded Austria that Poland should be reformed into a puppet state under full German control. They needed Poland to become a war machine that would provide Germany with men and supplies.

On November 5, 1916, Germany officially declared Poland a constitutional monarchy. In reality, this new monarchy was ruled only by the provisional council, which had no major powers. They acted as consultants to the German government on the Polish question. The Polish Kingdom created in 1916 had no fixed borders and no king to rule it. Piłsudski became the head of the Polish military, but he told the German government he would recruit a true army only when Poland became a true state. Germany was not ready to make such a big concession.

Dmowski's lobbying in France and Great Britain finally yielded results in 1917. Russian Tsar Nicholas II, under the pressure of his allies, finally agreed to make the restoration of an independent and united Poland one of the aims of the war. The Russian view on

Polish statehood didn't change even after the February Revolution, in which Tsar Nicholas II abdicated and transferred rule to the Russian Provisional Government. It didn't change even when Vladimir Lenin and his Bolsheviks raised the October Revolution (1917) and transferred governmental power into the hands of the Soviets.

However, the Bolsheviks were ready to end the war and sign a treaty with Germany, separate from their allies, Great Britain and France. In light of these new events, Berlin changed its stance toward its goals in the east. The German government recognized the statehood of Ukraine and Lithuania. The Russians were ready to admit defeat, and a treaty was signed on March 3, 1918. This also meant that the Bolsheviks were ready to give up on Poland. Berlin was ready to extend its Reich into Polish territory once under Russian control. But the future of Poland wasn't exclusively in the hands of Germany.

Dmowski worked on very energetic campaigns throughout Europe, advocating Polish independence. He had the help of famous Polish pianist, composer, and spokesman Ignacy Jan Paderewski, who toured the US and met President Woodrow Wilson, whom he convinced to support Polish unification and independence. When President Wilson issued his Fourteen Points, he demanded Polish independence and Poland's access to the sea. His statement would become the main principle for the peace negotiations that would conclude the Great War. In June of 1918, the Entente endorsed the idea of independent Poland as one of their war goals. The Poles didn't passively wait to see the outcome of the war: they volunteered in the French army, where General Józef Haller commanded the Polish Legion.

As the war neared its end, the situation in Poland changed. The breakup of Austria-Hungary allowed the Poles to take control over southeastern (Cieszyn) Silesia and western Galicia. When the revolution started in Germany and the socialists took over the government on November 9, the German military garrison station in Warsaw was evacuated. Thus, the last obstacle to the establishment of independence was removed. Inspired by the development of events, Poznanian Poles took up arms against their German rulers and freed themselves.

The three empires that partitioned Poland were no more, but united Poland didn't simply happen overnight. Politically and socially, Poland was as divided as ever. In the following days, a series of dramatic events would decide the fate of the new Polish state. Józef Piłsudski spent sixteen months in a German prison for his disobedience and refusal to create the Polish army. Now released, he gained the support of the Poles, who saw him as a hero who had fought for national freedom. The Regency Council that Germany put in power in September of 1917 proclaimed Piłsudski commander-in-chief of the army on November 11, 1918. Three days later, the council dissolved itself. November 11 is still celebrated as Poland's Independence Day. Lublin soon recognized the authority of Piłsudski, making him head of the state, and he would stay in the office until 1922. He became the father of the Second Polish Republic and would remain a dominant political figure and diplomat until he died in 1935.

The Second Republic

Józef Piłsudski had a very strong position within the new Republic of Poland. He enjoyed the support of socialists and the peasant parties and was approved by the Regency Council. He nominated Jędrzej Moraczewski as Prime Minister of the Republic and the head of the government. Moraczewski was extremely loyal to Piłsudski—and he was a socialist. His left-wing government introduced a series of reforms and welfare measures, including the eight-hour workday. He also promoted compulsory land reform. However, the National Democrats in Poznan refused to recognize Moraczewski's government in Warsaw. The SDKPiL merged with its allies to form the Communist Worker's Party of Poland and refused to recognize the Second Polish Republic and independence.

Because political division in Poland continued, industry was paralyzed and unemployment grew. Communication had remained disrupted since the war, and agricultural production was dramatically low. Poverty and famine took over the land. All was not well in the new state. It didn't help that there were no fixed frontiers this early in the Republic's existence. In eastern Galicia, Ukrainians fought the Poles over control of Lwow. The border with Russia remained fluid as the Red Army continuously tried to seize territory abandoned by the Germans. The border between Poland and Germany was not determined, as it would be decided during the Versailles peace conference.

Piłsudski realized he could keep the Polish unified and independent only if he made peace with the National Democrats, especially because the Entente powers never agreed to recognize his leadership and Moraczewski's government but supported the Polish National Committee in Paris. Moraczewski had to be replaced with someone ND would support, someone who could bridge the differences between the opposed political parties. That someone was the pianist Ignacy Jan Paderewski, who had already proved his loyalty to Poland by lobbying for its independence. But Paderewski wasn't enough. Piłsudski needed democratic parliamentary elections that would secure the cooperation of the ND. The elections held in 1919 were based on universal suffrage and produced a fragmented but balanced Sejm. The ND won just over a third of the parliamentary seats, while the center (peasant PSL Piast Party) and left (all the left-wing parties, including peasants) each won around 30 percent of the seats. The Communists called for a boycott of the elections, but they were largely ignored.

The new Sejm adopted the so-called "small" constitution in February 1919. This constitution was modeled on that of the French Third Republic. This meant that the Sejm would elect the head of the state, and all the ministers were responsible to the parliament. Piłsudski remained head of the state, but the new constitution limited his powers. He also remained the commander-in-chief, which gave him a tremendous influence on the state. Within several months since Poland had gained independence, Piłsudski managed to create a large national army—a remarkable achievement given the short time he was in power. After the democratic elections, France, Britain, and Italy recognized the Polish Second Republic.

The Treaty of Versailles, signed on June 28, 1919, officially ended the Great War. Poland managed to negotiate direct (though very narrow) access to the Baltic Sea. The Treaty transferred Poznania and most of Pomerania (west Prussia) to the new Polish Republic. However, Poland had to give up its historic city of Danzig (Gdansk), as the Germans made up most of its population. Danzig became a free city, though it fell under the Polish customs area. In the southeast, the Polish occupied Western Galicia, a Ukrainian territory. However, they would not be able to hold this territory for long, as Ukraine gained international support, especially from the Entente powers. The border with Russia represented a major issue. This area was in the midst of a civil war, as the various ethnic minorities that lived there wanted to overthrow the Bolshevik rule.

The ND called for the annexation of western Ukraine, Belarus, and Lithuania because although the Poles were a minority there, these territories were economically valuable. But Piłsudski believed that federalization would be a better solution than outright annexation. All these territories had a common enemy, Russia, which should have been reason enough to unite them. Piłsudski tried to make an east European federation with Polish leadership. This federation would encompass Poland, Belarus, Ukraine, and the Baltic states. But Polish and Lithuanian nationalists rejected the idea of a federation in favor of national states. Piłsudski realized he could still achieve the federation, though he would have to drag Poland into a war with Russia.

The Polish government quickly recognized Ukraine's independence and allied with them against the Red Army. They launched the offensive against Russia on April 25, 1920, and by May 7, they entered Kyiv. Their victory was short-lived, as the Poles underestimated the strength of the Bolsheviks. The Russians attacked at once from both north and south and pushed the Poles into a retreat. The Red Army continued advancing towards Warsaw, but they were not as welcomed as the Communists believed they would be. Instead, their passing through many Polish villages only caused the peasants to revolt. Piłsudski then used this revolt to raise an army of thousands of volunteers, peasants, students, and workers. They organized a counterattack from August 16 to 18, 1920, against the Bolshevik lines advancing from the south.

The Polish cryptographers were able to decipher all Russian communications, which gave them an enormous advantage in the upcoming battle. They even disrupted the enemy's radio signals and transmitted verses from the Book of Genesis. The Battle of Komarów, which took place between August 20 and September 2, is considered the last great European battle in which cavalry was used the old-fashioned way. (Soon, it would be turned into mounted infantry.) Both the Polish and Russian armies had around 20,000 horsemen, but the Poles used the confusion and disorientation of the Red Army to push its cavalry into a retreat. In the subsequent battle at the Niemen River, the Polish confirmed their victory. By the end of October, the Polish army entered Minsk, where the peace talks were already in progress.

The Polish-Soviet border was determined after the war with the signing of the Peace of Riga on March 18, 1921. The Polish-Soviet war officially ended, and Ukrainian and Belarusian territories were divided between Russia and Poland. With the betrayal of their

Ukrainian allies, Piłsudski's idea of a federation was ruined. In 1920, the Polish also tried to take back Lithuania by occupying the city of Wilno, where most of the population were Poles and Jews. Piłsudski even proposed a new union with Lithuania inside his federation, but modern Lithuania followed the ideology of ethnic nationalism and refused to enter the federation. When they lost Wilno, the Lithuanians established a new capital in Kaunas and proclaimed a formal state of war with Poland, though no further fighting ever happened. They would claim to be at war with their neighbors until 1938.

The new Polish border in the east was officially recognized in March 1923 at the Conference of Ambassadors in Paris. Most of the Polish population found themselves within the borders of their country. But a third of Poland's population consisted of various other minorities—including Jews, Lithuanians, Russians, Ukrainians, and Latvians. The Peace of Riga secured peace in eastern Europe, but not for long. A new war would ravage the land once again in less than two decades. Many of the minorities of Poland fought for their national interests. During the interwar period, Poland remained in good relations only with Latvia and Romania of all its neighbors. But peace persisted despite the heightened tensions.

Poland in World War II

Old Town in Warsaw after the destruction of the city by Germans in 1944
https://en.wikipedia.org/wiki/Destruction_of_Warsaw#/media/File:Destroyed_Warsaw,_capital_of_P oland,_January_1945_-_version_2.jpg

During the twenty-year interwar period, Poland raised a new generation to which independence was the norm. The country was developing fast and bridging over the social, cultural, and economic differences between provinces that were for so long parts of other countries. The railway network was expanded to connect these provinces, and the national airline LOT was established. Government institutions, laws, and civil service functioned effectively across the country. The education system was still not spread equally, and illiteracy was high in the eastern countries—although reduced from the previous 33 percent to 15 percent. Those who received higher education proved its quality: Poland produced renowned academics and scientists, especially mathematicians.

But the overall living standard of the Polish people wasn't high. It was especially low in the countryside, where unemployment affected over five million people. The Polish economy developed fast, but not fast enough to secure the country's military and economic supremacy over its neighbors, Germany and Russia. With Hitler's rise to power, Poland's time was running out. The Nazi leader was adamant about rejecting the Treaty of Versailles, the same treaty that recognized independent Poland. Other European powers tried to avoid war, and Polish leaders were disheartened once they realized France and Britain would not respond to Hitler's provocations.

At first, Poland gave the impression it was working with the neighboring dictators, as it forced Lithuania to establish diplomatic relations with the government in Warsaw. Poland also annexed Cieszyn, a disputed territory under the control of Czechoslovakia. But Poland acted out of fear of war, especially after Germany annexed Austria in 1938. The final goal of the Polish foreign minister, Józef Beck, was to create an eastern block between Russia and Germany that would consist of Hungary, Romania, Poland, and Polish-controlled Slovakia. But the annexation of Cieszyn wasn't the right approach, and Beck failed to realize this eastern block. Strained relations with Lithuania further corroded the relations between Poland and the Baltic states.

Hitler wanted to prey on Poland and make it a German vassal state. However, his initial plan was to dominate Poland as a weaker ally. Poland was already nurturing its own Nazi group and was oriented towards anti-Communism, anti-Russia, and anti-Semitism. It is no wonder Germany thought Poland would be an easy target and perhaps even a willing ally. This is why Germany asked Poland to join the Anti-Comintern Pact it created with Japan in 1936. The goal of this pact was to fight international Communism and its spread. But when Poland refused, Berlin asked for the return of Danzig and the creation of an extraterritorial highway and railway across Polish Pomerania (this territory was also called the Polish Corridor) that would connect Germany with Eastern Prussia, its exclave.

France and Britain tried to appease Nazi Germany by backing out of the agreement to defend Czechoslovakia. When Hitler occupied Prague in March of 1939, Poland knew it was next.

However, the Polish leaders didn't give in to panic because now Britain and France had to react. By occupying Prague, Germany broke the Munich agreement by which it had previously promised it would not expand its territory in Czechoslovakia beyond German-speaking Sudetenland. On March 26, 1939, the Polish government declined Hitler's offer of an alliance, and on March 31, Britain promised that it would defend Poland if Germany attacked it. The great European powers could no longer stand by and observe Hitler's expansion.

Infuriated, Hitler started planning the attack on Poland. He demanded the full occupation in only six weeks, but the Wehrmacht (unified German army) leaders warned him it would take at least three months to subdue Poland. The German diplomatic efforts strived to isolate Poland from its allies, Britain and France, but when Hitler signed the Nazi-Soviet Pact with the USSR, Britain and Poland signed a formal alliance. Still, Hitler refused to believe that the western powers would fight for Poland. Britain hoped the situation could still be salvaged by talking and persuaded the Polish government to delay mobilization. When Nazi Germany attacked on September 1, 1939, Poland was not ready. However, the French and British declaration of war on Germany two days later came as a surprise for Hitler.

Poland fought back. It didn't want to become a German satellite state, and it counted on the help of its new allies, Britain and France. But the September efforts tested Polish strength to its limits. Alone and only partially mobilized, it never stood a chance against the mighty Nazi war machine. The Germans applied their "blitzkrieg" tactics with enormous effect, but Poland continued to resist however it could. Its small but brave air force fought the far more superior Luftwaffe (German air force). On September 9, Poland launched a counteroffensive west of Warsaw. The battle took place on the Bzura river, and in the next three days, Germany lost five divisions. Around 50,000 German soldiers died, and 500 airplanes and 1,000 armored vehicles were destroyed. But Poland paid a great price. Its sacrifice numbered 200,000 soldiers and an unknown (but certainly great) number of civilian victims.

Polish troops planned to retreat and redoubt in the southeast, close to the border with Romania. But on September 17, 1939, Soviet troops attacked Poland from the east, sealing the fate of the Second Republic. Warsaw resisted until September 27, and the army continued fighting both Germans and Soviets until October 5, the day Hitler entered Warsaw in his victory parade. The Nazi-Soviet agreement divided Poland equally along the Narva, Bug, and San rivers. Germans thus gained the more populated and richer part of Poland. Yet again, the Polish state ceased to exist. However, that doesn't mean the Polish people simply surrendered. Most of its army managed to cross the border with Hungary and Romania and join foreign forces in their fight against Nazi Germany. Even the Polish navy left the Baltic sea and joined the British.

The Polish government refused to surrender. The high command escaped to Romania, but to their surprise, they were interned there. The French pressed Polish president Ignacy Mościcki to proclaim a moderate politician, Władysław Raczkiewicz, as his successor. At the start of the war, Raczkiewicz had escaped to France and was able to establish a new government-in-exile there. This government was recognized by the Allied Powers and endorsed by France and Britain. This meant that constitutionally, the government-in-exile was legal. Commander-in-chief Władysław Sikorski started forming a Polish army in France, which would establish contact with the resistance groups back in Poland.

The USSR immediately annexed the eastern part of Poland except Wilno (Vilnius), which they gave to Lithuania. Key figures of the Polish military, politics, civil servants, and trade union leaders were arrested. The rest of the population was terrorized into obedience. Land was confiscated, political, social, and cultural organizations were dissolved, and both private and public enterprises were shut down. The Russians also introduced conscription into the Red Army and imposed Soviet-style collectivization. Between 1940 and 1941, most of the Polish and Jewish population from the eastern part were deported to Central Asia and Siberia, where they were forced to labor in Gulags. Thousands of Polish and Jewish families perished in the inhospitable conditions of their places of exile.

Stalin and other Soviet leaders denied the atrocities committed upon the population of eastern Poland during the USSR occupation and annexation. But all who were deemed untruthful were either deported or simply killed. Mass killings of civil servants, Polish officers, and even border guards were the norm. Over 21,000 people were shot only in 1940. But while the Soviets proved merciless to those they considered enemies, they always sought to recruit Poles willing to cooperate, especially the left-wing intellectuals. The policy of winning over the Polish people gained momentum after the fall of France in June 1940. Hitler announced he planned to attack the USSR next as part of his Lebensraum plan (expanding Nazi dominion to create "living space" for his people).

The Nazis surpassed the Soviets in terrorizing Poland. The Nazi occupation lasted longer and extended the entirety of pre-war Poland. Most of the people suffered under the Nazi regime, and the death toll was far greater than in USSR-controlled eastern parts of the country. A large part of western Poland, including Łódź and Poznań, was annexed by the Third Reich. The population was classified according to their "race." Those classified as Germans, mostly from Upper Silesia and Pomerania, fell under the German military conscription law. The people classified as Poles were deprived of all property and education (except the most basic) and were forced into labor or deportation. They represented the underclass of the Nazi German society.

All Polish Catholic churches, charities, and organizations were closed, and the German language was enforced in the religious sphere. The central part of Poland was separately administered by the Nazi-founded General Government. In 1941, eastern Galicia was added to this administrative unit. The people of central Poland were exposed to daily terrors committed by the German military. They were starved and exploited physically and economically. All unwanted Poles and Jews from the territory of the Third Rich were deported here. The cultural life of Poland was completely closed down under the excuse of "spiritual sterilization." Theaters, museums, libraries, concert halls, and various cultural organizations were closed down, and playing Chopin's music was forbidden. The people were given basic education and technical training that would enable them to work. The only form of entertainment was a cinema, and even there, the people were constantly bombarded by Nazi propaganda.

Most Polish intellectuals were rounded up and imprisoned in concentration camps. They were also victims of mass executions. The first to suffer such a fate were the staff of Krakow University in 1939. Some of them were Jews, but most of them were Polish people. Doctors, lawyers, engineers, teachers, and clergy were ruthlessly exterminated. The rest of the Polish population were turned into slaves and were forced to labor. Between 1939 and 1944, more than 2.2 million Poles were relocated to Germany to perform compulsory work. Public shootings and executions became the norm. Germany introduced a law that for every German murdered in the territory of ex-Poland, 100 Polish people were to be executed. Polish children who had "racially appropriate" features were taken away from their parents and Polish orphanages to be brought up as Aryans in the homes of Nazi Germans. The end goal for Poland was to become a Nazi territory and for the Polish people to be either exterminated or expelled into the Soviet territory.

But however vicious the treatment of the Polish was, Jews and the Gypsies suffered a catastrophe. Nazis considered them to be subhuman, and they were often subjected to mass killings and imprisonment in the ghettos. The largest was the Warsaw ghetto, with over 450,000 souls imprisoned there. After 1941, when the Nazis took over the eastern part of Poland, they were able to get their hands on even more Jews. In 1942, the Nazis held the Wannsee Conference, during which they decided that all Jews of occupied Europe should be deported to Poland and killed. To implement this genocide, the Nazis built a system of death camps across Poland, the most famous of which is Auschwitz-Birkenau, followed by Treblinka and Majdanek. By the end of 1944, around 90 percent of the three million Jewish Poles perished in these camps.

Poles reacted differently to the Nazi treatment of the Jews. Some people exploited the Jewish misfortunes and looked to profit from them. Informants would collect payment for betraying Jews to the Nazis, and some extreme-right nationalists even started killing Jews. Most of the population was indifferent to the suffering of their Jewish neighbors, but this was due to Nazi propaganda and the introduction of death penalties for anyone who helped Jews in any way. The sight of mass executions that became so common after 1941 added to the adopted indifference. Among the Polish population, peasants were most willing to help the unfortunates no matter what religion or ethnicity they belonged to. In fact, many Poles were willing to help across the countryside and in towns and cities. They offered sanctuary to the Jews, produced false papers, or even organized their escape across the border. The convents often accepted Jewish children, assimilating them into the Catholic and Polish way of life just so their lives would be saved. All in all, around 45,000 Jews managed to escape Poland from the beginning of the war until 1944.

When France fell in 1940, the Polish government-in-exile moved to Great Britain. They were followed by 20,000 Polish soldiers that agreed to fight under British command. These soldiers were put to use in 1941 when they helped defend Tobruk in Libya during the siege that lasted for 241 days. Polish pilots proved their worth during the Battle of Britain (July 10-October 30, 1940), when they took down 200 Nazi planes out of the 1,977 aircraft destroyed. The Polish navy fought alongside the British one in the Atlantic and Mediterranean. But the most significant achievement of the Polish army was the excellent intelligence that it happily shared with Britain and France. In 1939, the Polish army provided the Allies with a replica of the Enigma machine, the Nazi coding system. Although the world celebrates Alan Turing for cracking the Enigma code, the truth is he would never have been able to do it without the help of three Polish mathematicians— Marian Rejewski, Jerzy Różycki, and Henryk Zygalski. These three cryptographers are rarely mentioned outside of Poland, but in their country, they are celebrated as heroes who helped shorten the war by at least two years.

Resistance groups back in Poland started emerging as early as 1939. There were many different groups, but since 1940, their work was coordinated by General Stefan Rowecki. The Polish resistance reached its maximum size by mid-1944, when it numbered over 400,000 members. The largest underground organization went by the name Armia Krajowa (AK for short), which translates to the Home Army. It wasn't the largest only in Poland but in all of Europe. Eventually, all other Polish resistance groups came under the wing of the AK—all except the Communist-led Peoples Army (AL) and the ultra-nationalist National Armed Forces (NSZ). The AK focused on gathering intelligence and organizing propaganda during the early years of World War II. Slowly, they started indulging in punishing the collaborators and planning and executing many sabotages. In early 1943, the AK increased its military activity and started planning a nationwide insurrection.

During the early years of the war, Poland had little to no chances of gaining its independence soon. But when Germany attacked the USSR in June of 1941 and Japan bombed Pearl Harbor, dragging the US into the war, Poland's fate was about to change—though not in the way the Polish people hoped. Once again, the fate of their country lay in the hands of global powers, and it was on foreigners to decide how Poland should continue its existence. When Britain signed an alliance with the USSR on July 13, 1941, Prime Minister Winston Churchill pressed the Polish government-in-exile to sign a treaty with the Soviets. The so-called Sikorski-Maisky agreement was signed on July 30, 1941, annulling the Soviet-Nazi partitioning of Poland from 1939. The Soviets had to release the Polish prisoners, and the USSR had to form a Polish army on its territory.

For Stalin, these concessions to Poland were only temporary. Sikorski hoped that the Polish army fighting under British command would help liberate Poland and that USSR would acknowledge Polish sovereignty. But Stalin refused to make any promises to respect the pre-war Polish-Soviet border. He also wasn't willing to supply the Polish army created within the USSR. They had to be shipped to Iran, where they joined the British effort. Moscow also failed to explain what happened to the tens of thousands of Polish officers and civilians captured in 1939 and shipped to the Gulags. All of this led to the failure of the Sikorski-Maisky agreement. Sikorski lost his influence in Poland, while the leader of the Peasant Party (PSL), Stanisław Mikołajczyk, gained popularity. In 1943, he became the Prime Minister of the government-in-exile, replacing Władysław Sikorski.

To achieve his goals with Poland, Stalin started promoting his influence. He encouraged the establishment of the Communist Party in Poland in 1942, now renamed the Polish Workers' Party (PPR). In 1943, the party was under the leadership of Władysław Gomułka, a Moscow-trained Communist. The Communists not only refused to recognize the Polish government-in-exile but also started to claim they represented the real interest of the Polish nation. Stalin approved the creation of a new Polish army, this time under the leadership of Communists willing to cooperate with the USSR. The new Polish army would see its first battle in the territory of Belarus in 1943. Furthermore, Stalin suspended diplomatic relations with Poland in April 1943 once the USSR was accused of committing atrocities upon 4,000 Polish officers in Katyn.

The realities of war led the Allies to give precedence to their alliance with the USSR over Polish interests. At the Allied conference in Teheran held from November 28 to December 1, 1943, they decided that the Polish eastern border should be formed at the Curzon Line (the border drawn after World War I), but with Lviv and Vilnius going into Soviet hands. Poland would receive some territories in the west at the expanse of Germany. This decision was made by US President Franklin Roosevelt, British Prime Minister Winston Churchill, and USSR leader Joseph Stalin. The Polish were not invited to the conference and did not influence the matter. The Poles wanted the same borders in the east as pre-1939 and territorial compensation from Germany for human losses and material damage committed by the Nazi regime.

The Red Army entered Polish territory on July 21, 1944, defeating the Germans. In eastern Poland, a Soviet-backed Polish Committee of National Liberation (PKWN) claimed to be the government of liberated Poland as opposed to the underground state run by the AK (Home Army). As the Red Army approached Warsaw, the AK needed to act fast and liberate the capital so it could establish an independent Polish administration without the Soviet's involvement. On August 1, 1944, the AK launched an attack on the Nazis in Warsaw. They believed it would take only a few days to liberate the city, but they were extremely unequipped, and the fighting prolonged for two months. At that time, Stalin halted the advance of the Red Army at the Vistula river and waited for the Nazis to finish off the AK soldiers. Soviet-sponsored Polish troops tried to cross the river and help their compatriots in the fight, but they had no support from the Red Army. Their effort failed.

The scene in Warsaw was a disaster. The fighting there is considered one of the bloodiest and most savage urban battles of World War II. The city capitulated on October 2, with over 17,000 soldiers and more than 200,000 civilians dead. Hitler's vengeance was brutal, as he wanted the city obliterated. The remaining population was drawn out of Warsaw so the city could be systematically destroyed. More than 80 percent of the city was razed to the ground, including all the museums, parks, theaters, churches, castles, and historical buildings. Suffering this excruciating loss, the AK felt obliged to capitulate. The Poles now had no other choice but to accept the PKWN leadership. The Soviet-Polish army absorbed all the Polish fighters and grew to number 400,000 men before it joined the Soviet attack on Germany.

Chapter 9 – Poland, Communism, and the Cold War

The Palace of Culture and Science in Warsaw, a symbol of Communist power in Poland
Romák Éva, CC BY-SA 3.0;
https://en.wikipedia.org/wiki/History_of_Poland#/media/File:A_Kult%C3%BAra_%C3%A9s_Tudom
%C3%A1ny_Palot%C3%A1lja._Fortepan_75020.jpg

New Polish State

Stalin's influence grew in Poland quickly, and he now planned to make a legal government out of the PKWN. But to make the Communist, society-controlled government acceptable to the people, he had to add some democratic elements from the government-in-exile in London. The PKWN proclaimed itself the Provisional Government of the Republic of Poland on December 31, 1944, with the full support of the USSR. The United States and Britain continued to recognize the Polish government-in-exile, but they were more eager to keep their relations with the USSR than to help Poland develop into a democratic and independent state. The government-in-exile ceased being relevant to the Polish question and had no say in the future of its country. At the Yalta Conference of February 1945, Stalin, Roosevelt, and Churchill confirmed their decision to draw the Polish eastern border roughly following the Curzon Line. Many Poles consider Yalta to be the ultimate betrayal of their western allies.

The New Polish Provisional Government of the National Unity was established at the conference in the Kremlin, where six non-Communist politicians were added to the previous PKWN government. Among them was Stanisław Mikołajczyk, ex-prime minister from the Peasants' Party. He now took the role of deputy prime minister, while the office of prime minister was given to the pro-Soviet socialist Edward Osóbka-Morawski. Only a few hundred yards away, at the same time as the conclusion of the Kremlin conference, the leaders of the underground government and the AK resistance movement were tried for being members of the illegal organizations and for collaborating with Germans. Sixteen men who were tried had been previously kidnapped from Warsaw by the NKVD, the social security service. Between 1944 and 1947, around 50,000 Poles, most members of the ex-AK resistance, were arrested and imprisoned in the Soviet Gulags. Britain and the US withdrew their recognition of the Polish government-in-exile on July

5, 1945, but it continued existing until 1990 with the symbolic role of bearing witness to the violence committed upon Poland during the Second World War.

Despite the popular belief of many Poles, Stalin had no intention of annexing Poland or incorporating it in any way into the USSR. But Poland was geographically very important to Russia, as it was on its direct path to Berlin and Soviet-controlled eastern Germany. Although Poland was allowed statehood, it needed to be under direct and complete control of the USSR. Any resistance to the Soviets had to be immediately crushed. Admission of non-Soviet Mikołajczyk into the provisional government and the promise of democratic elections were simply disguises for the full control the Communists had over Poland.

Poland did gain the promised compensation for its eastern border in the form of ex-German territories, but the Poles never dreamed they would gain the whole of Silesia and Pomerania. Surprisingly, it wasn't the provisional government that pushed to get these territories during the Potsdam Conference that took place from July to August 1945. It was the Soviets who demanded this large compensation so they could assert full control over Poland. One day, if Germany demanded these territories back, Poland would have to rely on the USSR for defense. Polish Communists endorsed this expansion to the west, as they saw it as the return to the borders of Piast Poland and only strengthened their position to demand a homogenous nation-state.

Nazi ethnic cleansing took a reverse course, and around eight million Germans were expelled from Silesia, Pomerania, and Easter Prussia. German settlement east of the Oder river ended after seven centuries of existence. The Soviets insisted on settling these parts with the Poles from the east, from the territory that now belonged to the USSR. Most of the Poles from Lviv were uprooted and deported to the west to settle the ruined city of Breslau, now renamed Wrocław. The Polish population of Wilno (Vilnius) was also moved so it could become a USSR and Lithuanian city. Life in the new Polish west was not easy, as most of it had been destroyed during the war, and what little was left was looted by the Communist opportunists. Around 1.5 million Poles who had been sent to Germany for forced labor finally returned home.

The Polish people within and outside of their country were generally not happy with the outcome of the war. Even though they remained an independent sovereign state, they had been betrayed by their allies and left to the mercy of Soviet Russia.

After the Second World War, a new Polish state emerged. It was not only territorially different from the previous Second Republic but also demographically, politically, and socially different. Poland's shape and geographical position were dramatically different, as it lost territories in the east but gained some in the west and north. The new state was smaller by 20 percent, but it acquired a 300-mile-long (483 km) coast opening the country to the Baltic Sea. Although the newly-acquired territories were devastated after the war, they were much more developed than the lost eastern ones. The demographic changes were a direct result of the war and its atrocities. In 1939, Poland had around thirty-five million people, but after the war, that number dropped to twenty-four million. However, the population was now overwhelmingly Polish. Poland's social and political life was obliterated by war, death, and the displacement of people.

Poland was the country most affected by the war. The devastation in other European countries cannot even be compared to what happened in Poland. Whole cities were razed to the ground; people were mass murdered, displaced, starved, and tortured. After the war, famine and various infectious diseases took hold of a population already filled with invalids and orphans. There were not enough houses for all, as the Nazi Germans had destroyed most of the habitable places.

The new Polish state was under the USSR's firm political and military control. The Communists occupied all the key governmental offices, while the Soviet Security Service (NKVD), backed by the Red Army, had a full grip over the country. The Communist PPR had no support from the population, and its leaders knew they would never win the democratic elections promised by Stalin after the war. They needed time to consolidate their power and win over the Polish citizens. They also needed a mass membership. To achieve this, they mobilized and united the nation in the efforts to rebuild the country. It was the perfect timing to adopt a patriotic narrative and promise a Piast Poland to the population. The Provisional Government of National Unity adopted some very pragmatic policies considering the economic reconstruction of the country, culture, society, and religion.

In the early days of Polish Communism, political issues were heavily censored, but not much else. Publishing, arts, radio broadcast, and newspapers were permitted, and they worked regularly. There was no ideological supervision in Poland during the early post-war period. Schools were also permitted to return to the old educational curriculum and system, and the universities were reopened. Education was promoted, and the network of newly-opened schools was ever-growing. The church was allowed full freedom of worship, and a new parochial structure was established for the one million Poles settled in the western, previously German Protestant territories. Poland was now a fully Catholic country. The Communist authorities had to be very careful in their management of the church because Polish identity was always closely tied to Catholicism. It became even more so after the Second World War, as the suffering the clergy's experience was identical to that of the Polish population. It was even easier for the people to relate to the church now than before 1939.

The anti-Communist guerilla groups fought for supremacy in Soviet-controlled Poland. They hoped that the war between the

USSR and the western powers would come immediately after the Second World War, and they persisted in their resistance against the Communist establishment until 1947. The struggle for political power was violent, and it often led to bloodshed—even civil war. Up to 30,000 people lost their lives in the efforts against the new regime. Anti-Semitism continued during these unsettled times, partially because the Jews who survived the Holocaust demanded back their homes and businesses in Poland. Some Jews also joined the Communist government, hoping to regain their previous possessions. But the result was only exaggerated hatred towards the Jews from the opposition. Many Jews decided to leave Poland in the post-war years.

But the greatest danger for the Communists was the newly reconstructed Polish Peasant Party (PSL), with Stanisław Mikołajczyk at its head. The PSL was by far more popular than the Communists, and it gathered around one million members. The Communists and Soviets had to delay the promised democratic elections. To achieve this, they resorted to intimidation, violence, and even electoral fraud. On June 30, 1946, a national referendum was held relating to the abolishment of the senate and approval of the government's economic policies. The Communists took control of the electoral commissions and directly altered the results of the referendum. They claimed that over 68 percent of the population voted in support of all propositions, which gave the Communist PPR legitimacy. The real figure discovered much later in the records of the PPR was only 27 percent.

Communism in Power

The general elections were finally organized on January 19, 1947. But in their campaign, the Soviet authorities arrested and incarcerated thousands of PSL activists and hundred of their candidates, claiming they were working against the Polish nation and state. The elections were again falsified, and the official result claimed that the PPR gained 80 percent of the votes while PSL was given only 10 percent. Recent research proved that even with the intimidation and the violence committed upon PSL supporters, the Peasants' Party won between 60 and 70 percent of the votes. The free elections promised at the Yalta Conference proved to be a farse. The Communists were now free to take over Poland.

The new government was formed in February 1947, with Józef Cyrankiewicz as prime minister. Cyrankiewicz proved to be a very flexible politician. He started his career as a Socialist but transferred to Communist in 1948 to accommodate the new government. He served as Polish prime minister twice, from 1947 to 1952 and from 1954 to 1970. After his second term, he continued his political activity as a chairman of the Polish Council of State. Other key ministries were now solely in the hands of the Communists. Mikołajczyk was forced to flee the country, while the remaining members of the PSL became Communist sympathizers. The Peasants' Party was formally absorbed into the pro-Communist United Peasant Party (ZSL).

The years 1947 and 1948 were marked by the ever-worsening climate of the Cold War. Moscow tightened its grip on the satellite states of the USSR, forcing them to adopt the Soviet model in the spheres of politics, economy, and social control. The purging of the PPR and the Socialist PPS followed. Everyone who dared to deviate from the Polish road to socialism was immediately dismissed from his post and replaced with more adequate people. In 1948, the PPS was forced to unite with the PPR and form the Polish United Workers' Party (PZPR). This Communist party would stay in power in Poland until 1989. All other Polish political parties formed before or after World War II were either abolished or transformed into the satellite parties of the PZPR. Their role was symbolic, as they were kept separate so Poland could claim it was a democratic and politically pluralist country.

The new constitution, amended by Stalin, was issued in 1952, and with it, the Polish People's Republic was created. Industrial workers were labeled the leading class in Polish society, but everyone who wanted employment needed a PZPR membership card. Elections after 1952 became just a formality in which over 90 percent of the votes were given to the candidates of the PZPR. Stalin couldn't trust the Polish army, and in 1949, he started purging it of all native officers. By 1952, all generals and officers of the Polish army were citizens of the USSR. In the Polish territory annexed by the Soviets, Polish citizens were deprived of all their social, cultural, and religious institutions. They were not allowed to continue their education in the Polish language.

The population of the Polish Peoples' Republic was pressed hard by the security apparatus, which now numbered 200,000 officials. That is six times more than the Polish police forces before the war. The population was constantly intimidated, and all who stepped out of Communist lines were arrested. People started fearing the informants, as between 1945 and 1956, more than 5,000 death sentences were passed, all for political reasons. Tens of thousands of adults were arrested and served time in prisons and detention centers. The judicial system, trade unions, youth organizations, and press, came under the direct control of the Communists.

Poland was to follow the Soviet-style Six-Year Plan, by which the country would quickly be industrialized. The triumph of this program was the opening of the Lenin steel mill in Nowa Huta near Krakow. The state also provided a basic welfare system, but it favored the workers—those who contributed to the Polish industrial economy—while the elderly and rural population were put aside. The Six-Year Plan helped curb pre-war unemployment, although the wages were often not enough for a decent living. Peasants were uprooted from their farms and brought to cities to work in newly-founded factories. They were promised a bright proletarian future, but they only got common housing in workers' hostels, low wages, and long working hours. This led to a deficit of people who would take on agriculture and food production. The state started the collectivization of land, and by 1955, nearly a quarter of Poland's arable land belonged to state farms. Food production was so low that compulsory requisition and rationing had to be implemented.

The only remaining autonomous and national institution was the Catholic Church. But even the church couldn't escape the Communist fight against religion. In 1959, Pope Pius XII threatened to excommunicate all those who belonged to Communist organizations. The Vatican also refused to acknowledge the new western border of Poland and its new government. The pope continued to support the government-in-exile in London until 1956. The Communist leaders took the opportunity to start a campaign against the church and dissolve many of its charity organizations and activities. Religious teachings were banned from schools, hospitals, and the army, and church attendance was discouraged. The new government schemed to create a new national church and sever the ties with Rome, but that never came to pass. Instead, in 1953, the state assumed the power to control all church appointments and demanded an oath of loyalty from old and new clergy.

Stalin-style rule in Poland was totalitarian, but it never reached the scope it had in the Soviet Union. In fact, in 1955, the Polish United Workers' Party (PZPR) officially condemned the repressions committed by the party during the Stalinist period, which lasted until Stalin died in 1953. During the Congress of the Communist Party of the Soviet Union held in 1956, the secretary of the Communist Party of the Soviet Union, Nikita Khrushchev, publicly declared that a new era had started, in which there was no room for Stalinist repression. In Poland, the people pressed for a change. Public demonstrations took place in Poznań, where the crowd waved the national flag while singing religious songs. They demanded bread and freedom. The masses were only stopped by the army and tanks on the streets. Although the demonstrations were quickly quelled, they were a warning to the **PZPR** that Communism was in crisis.

A new leader, Władysław Gomułka, who had been imprisoned during the Stalinist period, was chosen to be president of the ex-Polish Workers' Party (PPR). He condemned the collectivization of land and the continuous dependence of Poland on the USSR. Everyone hoped Gomułka would bring change to the party and to Poland. But Moscow didn't agree with his election as the party president, although he had the support of Mao Zedong, a Chinese Communist leader.

Although openly against the Soviet Bloc, Gomułka couldn't move Poland out of it. Nevertheless, a milder form of Communist rule was set in place. The army was finally freed of USSR leadership, and new native officers were appointed. Security police were tamed and purged of the most notorious Stalinist torturers. Party leaders were changed on all levels, and the workers managed to remove hated factory directors. The collective farms were dissolved, and a compromise was reached with the church. Religious education was back in schools, and Catholic deputies were added to the parliament.

The foreign policies of the reformed **PZPR** changed, too. Gomułka persuaded Moscow to release some 200,000 Polish political prisoners from the war and post-war period. Travel to the USSR was eased for the citizens of Poland, and Moscow no longer enjoyed a favorable status when buying raw materials from Poland. The US also approached Poland, offering new diplomatic relations. In 1960, the US gave Poland the most favored nation (MFN) status in trade and opened its borders to Polish citizens. Gomułka's regime was taking Poland into a more prosperous future, and he gained the support of the majority of citizens. However, those who expected further liberalization were to find themselves greatly disappointed. Gomułka remained very hostile to the idea of democracy within the party, let alone in the country. The intellectuals, writers, and artists were still under heavy censorship and state control, and many of those who voiced opinions against the party or Communist rule were arrested, sentenced, or exiled.

In the sphere of the economy, Gomułka faired no better. He continued to insist on the heavy industrialization of Poland. Although there was no more collectivization, there were not enough food producers, and the population continued to suffer near-famine. Food shortages never stopped, and in the 1960s, the standard of living in Poland became worse than ever. The hard life circumstances and increasing censorship led to massive student protests in January 1968 in Warsaw. By March, the protests spread across the country, mostly in university cities. The masses of students expressing their liberal and anti-Russian sentiments were met by a violent response from the authorities. Although the protesters never managed to topple the government, they did ruin the good image of the Communist regime in Poland. The Marxist propaganda of the PZPR lost the support of the majority of the population. Gomułka's reputation suffered the most, and nothing he did in domestic or foreign policies ever made up for the police brutality committed upon the students. The Communists alienated an entire generation of young intellectuals.

In December of 1970, the Polish Communist government decided on a new economic reform program. The goal was to make some of the factories autonomous and introduce a new system of wage incentives. But the first phase of the program was to increase food prices, and the timing the Polish government chose to implement it only speaks to their incompetence. The increase in prices came unannounced on December 12, right before Christmas. It was a slap in the face for many Polish working families who were already spending more than three-fifths of their budget on food. Strikes started among the workers, first in the shipyards of Gdańsk (Danzig) and Gdynia. Police responded again with brutality and violence and even chose to gun down scores of workers in

Gdynia on December 17. Around forty workers were killed and more than a thousand wounded.

This event sparked a blaze of revolt across almost all of northern Poland. Moscow responded to the Polish troubles by demanding the dismissal of Gomułka, although the strikes were not the only reason. By this time, the Polish Communist leader had suffered a cerebral stroke and was forced to resign. Edward Gierek was appointed the First Secretary of the Party on December 20, 1970. However, this change in leadership didn't stop the strikes. They hit Poland with even greater determination in January 1971, and they wouldn't stop until Gierek personally appealed to the workers and promised reforms. To appease the citizens, he released some of the arrested workers that participated in the December strikes. Edward Gierek kept his promises and improved the workers' standard of living, lifted censorship, and invested in Polish cultural life, but he made no concessions toward the workers that demanded the creation of unions.

Giek abandoned Gomułka's policy of economic independence in Poland, which had served to expand and recover the failed economy of the previous government. Western credits started flowing into the country and quickly amounted to twenty-four billion dollars. New technology was introduced to Poland, and the country's production was finally able to step into the world market. The general standard of living of the population improved, especially once the government started dealing with the chronic housing shortage. Further investments were made in the car industry, and Fiat opened its first factories in Poland between 1970 and 1980. Foreign currency restrictions ended, and the Polish citizens were finally able to buy some of the goods made in western countries, previously unavailable in their Communist country.

The biggest achievement of Gierek's government was the abolition of the compulsory requisition of agricultural goods in 1945. It ended in 1971, allowing the peasants to finally gain independence and prosper. They were also brought into the social security system. However, the new government never bothered to change the foundations of the Polish economy. It still heavily relied on industry, and it was completely centralized. Many investments were wasted, as old industries that never underwent reform failed to produce quality items that would succeed in the foreign markets. By 1974, Gierek's economic success started taking a different turn. Inflation was on the rise, and the food shortages returned, making rationing a reality once again. Pressed by foreign debts and ever-growing inflation, the government had to increase prices in 1976, and another series of strikes and protests followed. However, this time the authorities refrained from using their guns against the protesters, and the brutality and violence were significantly lower.

The general unrest would continue in the 1980s as the economic situation in Poland continued to deteriorate. During the '80s, four-fifths of the Polish export income was dedicated to paying off foreign debt. The scale of the strikes wasn't as wide as those in the '70s, but the workers were determined. An inter-factory strike committee was organized, and by August 17, 1980, it issued twenty-one demands for the government. Among the demands were the organization of trade unions, the right to strike, and the right to freedom of expression. The Soviets advised Gierek to use force against the workers, but the Polish Communist leader refused to do it. The government finally approved the trade unions, and on September 17, "Solidarity," a national trade union, was founded. Its internal organization was democratic, and just in one month, it gathered over eight million members. Gierek's reputation among Communists suffered because of this concession to the workers, and he was removed from office and replaced by Stanisław Kania.

Solidarity was not an ordinary trade union. It quickly evolved into a social movement that wanted to democratize the political life of Poland. It became a political threat to the Communist monopoly in Poland and a direct threat to the unity of the Soviet Eastern Bloc.

Moscow had to react. There were even thoughts of invading Poland, but that would raise an international scandal and probably lead to another war that the USSR couldn't afford. Instead, the Soviet leadership demanded a crackdown on Solidarity. No matter how hard the Communist government tried to bring down Solidarity, the union persisted and even gained strength. This strength was demonstrated by the all-nation four-hour-long strike that took place on March 27, 1981. The peasants opened their branch of Solidarity, and by June, it was legalized. The inability of the PZPR to deal with this problem only served to show that its power was in decline. Of the party's three million members, a third abandoned it. Around 700,000 of these ex-members joined Solidarity.

When Solidarity announced a massive protest in Warsaw on December 17, 1981, the government responded by introducing martial law. The Polish army joined the security forces to maintain martial law, and even Soviet Marshal Kulikov came to supervise the situation in Poland. More than 6,000 Solidarity activists were arrested, together with their leader Lech Wałęsa, who spent eleven months in prison. The government militarized the factories, transportation, and communication. Strikes erupted all over the country, and again, brutal force was used to crush them. The military restored a semblance of public order, and the people returned to work and their daily lives. Although Solidarity was made illegal, its leadership, or what was left of it, reconstructed the organization underground. They launched a propaganda war against the authorities and the Communist government.

Lech Wałęsa became a Noble Prize Winner in October of 1983, which only enhanced his national and international reputation. After the crackdown on Solidarity and martial law, the party had no hopes of repairing its damaged image in society. The government even tried to win some of the people over by offering amnesty for the Solidarity members that were imprisoned, but to no avail. Martial law remained in place until June 1983. The next year, the PZPR allowed a foundation of a new national trade union as a counter to the outlawed Solidarity. It also assumed a patriotic stance, hoping to elicit national sentiment in the people and thus gain their support. Nothing was working, and the Communists found themselves in a political stalemate.

But the Communists hung on to power with an excruciating strength. They would not give in to the demands of Solidarity and the people, and when the strikes resumed in 1988, the government responded with force. But fearing they would cause a civil war, this time the PZPR decided against martial law. Communist Poland was bound to the Soviet Union not only by ideology but also by a constitutional partnership. One of the amendments in the Polish Communist constitution directly bound the two states together. However, the USSR was about to change its policy toward its satellite states. A renewed prospect of war with the US made the new Soviet leader, Mikhail Gorbachev, rethink the political system of the USSR.

As the Soviet grip on Poland was released, the Communist government had two choices: forcefully maintain control over the country or make a deal with the opposition, which would allow them to retain some degree of power and secure popular legitimacy. On August 26, 1988, talks between the government and opposition were proposed, to which Solidarity agreed. Lech Wałęsa met the interior minister, Czesław Kiszczak, on August 31, but the talks wouldn't take place for the next five months. In the meantime, Solidarity was made legal again.

The Polish Round Table Talks ended on April 5, 1989, with a compromise between the government and the opposition. There was to be a fundamental change in the Polish constitution. The offices of the president and the senate were now restored. The people would choose senate members in free elections, and the senate and Sejm would choose the president. The senate and the president would have the power to veto the parliament. The PZPR and their allies would have 65 percent of the parliament seats, while the freely elected representatives would hold 35 percent. The first semi-free elections took place on June 4, and they proved to be a disaster for the PZPR.

These elections proved to be the first move towards dismantling the Communist regime in Poland and central-eastern Europe. The Solidarity Citizens' Committee won all but one seat in the senate and all the free seats in the Sejm. On July 3, Gorbachev declared that Poland was now free to make decisions on its own and shape its future. Wojciech Jaruzelski, First Secretary of the PZPR, was elected the first president of Poland, ensuring that the Communists remained in power. However, the first prime minister was a Catholic intellectual, the Christian-democratic Tadeusz Mazowiecki. Although Lech Wałęsa chose to remain out of the offices for the time being, he would win the first free presidential elections in Poland after Jaruzelski resigned in 1990.

Conclusion

Poland transitioned from Communism to a democratic future without hitting any bumps in the road. Some wanted retaliation for the hardship caused by the Communist past, but most of the Polish people simply wanted to look forward and build their country anew. The Polish Third Republic started in 1989 with the first democratic elections, and all references to the Soviets and the Communists were erased from the constitution. But the newly democratic country still had far to go to catch up with its peers in western Europe. Its economy was in shambles and needed a wide-ranging program of reform. Of all the countries in the Eastern Bloc, Poland undertook the most radical reform, prepared by the new finance minister, Leszek Balcerowicz. He was responsible for making Poland a country with the fastest-growing economy at the time.

But the dismantling of the Communist economy and the restoration of the free enterprise and market inevitably led to the division of society. Ex-Communist officials gained from the privatization of state enterprises, while many workers who had helped bring Communism down now found themselves unemployed. Nevertheless, the standard of living was rising, with shops filled with goods of domestic and foreign origins. There were no more food shortages and rationings. Poland was entering a new chapter in history, suddenly free from its Soviet chains.

During the 1990s, Poland took the shape of a truly democratic country in which civil rights were restored, the military was depoliticized, and the culture was blooming. Western influence could be felt in everything, from new political life to movies and literature. Despite the way that Communism ended and the shape that modern Poland took (with borders that provoked some of its neighbors), no one could deny the country was finally free again, united, and wholly democratic. However, during World War II and all the years under the hard Soviet boot, Poland had been losing people. Many were self-exiled anti-Communists, war prisoners, or simply people who emigrated in search of a better life. For all these people who left, the Polish Third Republic came too late. Although some individuals returned, most emigree Poles had built their lives abroad and had no intention of returning. While they may have chosen to stay in foreign countries, they did mend their relationship with their motherland. They came to represent the Polish diaspora.

The political influence of the Catholic Church, that champion of ideological struggle and bastion of Polish nationality, continued to rise. Soon after the democratic elections of 1989, it became clear that its influence couldn't be ignored. The Catholic Church remains highly regarded in Polish society today. It is worth saying that a quarter of all the Catholic priests in Europe come from Poland. However, it seems that the same church that helped the country rise from its dark Communist past now stands in the way of modernization and prosperity. With its conservative outlook and propaganda, the Church has alienated many Poles—including Catholics. The church's warnings didn't dissuade the Poles from voting yes for a new democratic constitution in 1997. As a response, the Polish Church only became excessively defensive and even more conservative.

Poland joined the North Atlantic Treaty Organization (NATO) on March 12, 1999, together with Hungary and the Czech Republic. The Poles did so because they were conscious of their vulnerability, which had caused them hardship over the centuries. By joining an international defense organization, Poland secured a sense of security for its country. Only five years later, in 2004, Poland also joined the European Union, together with the Baltic neighbor with which it had once been united—Lithuania. Transitioning from an Eastern Bloc country to a member of the European Union, Poland was reaching forward, eager to assume its rightful place among the free countries of the world.

Here's another book by Captivating History that you might like

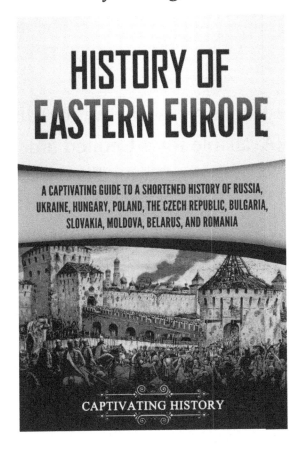

Free Bonus from Captivating History (Available for a Limited time)

Hi History Lovers!

Now you have a chance to join our exclusive history list so you can get your first history ebook for free as well as discounts and a potential to get more history books for free! Simply visit the link below to join.

Captivatinghistory.com/ebook

Also, make sure to follow us on Facebook, Twitter and Youtube by searching for Captivating History.

References

Dabrowski, P. M. (2021). *Poland: The First Thousand Years*. Cornell University Press.

Davies, N. (2013). *God's Playground: A History of Poland: In Two Volumes*. Oxford University Press.

Frost, R. (2018). *Oxford History of Poland-Lithuania: Volume I*. Oxford University Press.

Kochanski, H. (2014). *The Eagle Unbowed: Poland and the Poles in the Second World War*. Harvard University Press.

Lukowski, J., & Zawadzki, H. (2020). *A Concise History of Poland*. Cambridge University Press.

Moorhouse, R. (2020). *Poland 1939: The Outbreak of World War II*. Basic Books.

Nóra Berend, Urbanczyk, P., & Wiszewski, P. (2013). *Central Europe in the High Middle Ages: Bohemia, Hungary and Poland c. 900-c. 1300*. Cambridge University Press.

Roche, H. (2017). *Bloodlands: Europe between Hitler and Stalin*. Macat Library.

Wandycz, P. S. (1996). *The Lands of Partitioned Poland: 1795-1918*. University of Washington Press.

Zamoyski, A. (2018). *Poland: A History*. Hippocrene Books.

Made in the USA
Monee, IL
09 February 2023

27393216R00089